Uplifting Moments II

Wallace T. Davis

Copyright ©2021 Wallace T. Davis

All rights reserved. No part of this book may be reproduced in any form or by any electronic or mechanical means, including information storage and retrieval systems, without permission in writing from the publisher, except by reviewers, who may quote brief passages in a review.

Permissions for Bible quotations on last page.

ISBN 978-1-953406-21-7 Paperback

Cover design by Abigail Jackson
Interior graphic by Freepik

Printed in the United States of America

Published by Soncoast Publishing
P.O. Box 1503
Hartselle, AL 35640
www.soncoastpublishing.com

For over 20 years, Wallace T. Davis has inspired and motivated people through his Uplifting Moments, carried on four local radio stations during morning drive time. He is also featured on a local CBS affiliate on Sunday mornings.

Some of the best of these Uplifting Moments are collected in this daily devotional to provide you with encouragement, inspiration, and spiritual insight. This book has been published in hopes that your spirit and faith will grow to new heights as you read, meditate, and share these moments with others.

Preface

Uplifting Moments, created to be uplifting for our communities, has been aired on radio stations throughout the Gulf Coast of Alabama, Florida, and Mississippi for the past twenty-one years during daily 60 seconds "drive time." For the past four years, a CBS affiliate television station has broadcast these moments on Sunday mornings. When I began this outreach, my purpose was for people in our community to understand the values of Volunteers of America and learn a little about us and hopefully ignite their curiosity to know more. These moments have been effective in creating a connection with the community and opening up conversations and opportunities. God has blessed us, and we are grateful.

We intend to present *Uplifting Moments* in a setting where readers can use it as a part of their daily devotional time. In each reading, there is an appropriate Bible scripture, an uplifting moment, and an opportunity for you to talk with God and, perhaps, a friend.

Dr. Kevin Wilburn, my son-in-law, some time ago, suggested that I add Scripture to the *Uplifting Moments* and publish them as a devotional book. His suggestion germinated over the years, and we are now publishing the second volume!

I am grateful to those who have come along beside me during this journey. When I began to conceptualize this opportunity, George Myers helped me immensely and assisted in recording these moments. John Bell, the radio production manager for Clear Channel, was creative, patient, and supportive; he really made an impact! Ralph Mitchell, the production manager for IHeart Radio, took us to new levels and taught us how to develop Uplifting Moments in our home office studio. I appreciate our staff who worked closely with me at different times—Amanda Gonzales, Brooke Granade, Emily Pate, Henry Creel, and Jolyn Castillo. They were all supportive and helpful along the way.

There are no limits to caring ®

Dr. Paul McLendon and Dr. Rob Jackson assisted in selecting scriptures for each *Uplifting Moment*. Furthermore, I am thankful for Rob's valuable assistance, insight, and help in getting the book published.

My wife, Barbara, has been by my side throughout this journey. I am grateful for her love, support, insights, work, and who she is to me. She is also my editor, and she did the audio recording of these moments and made them sound much better than reality!

The covers for this book and the first volume were uplifting paintings from Barbara. *Uplifting Moments II* cover is the place I proposed marriage to her. After asking the question three different ways, she said, "Yes!" The first book cover was from a painting that she did of us in Yosemite National Park.

I am thankful for the many people who have inspired and stimulated me along the way to develop these *Uplifting Moments*. There are those I don't know who have contributed to these moments... for you, a special "thank you." It is impossible to acknowledge all those who gave an illustration. Some stories were on the internet or public domain. Others were stories I have picked up through a lifetime of work. It was not my intention to infringe on anyone's copyright but simply to share an uplifting moment of the best I've seen along my way.

Wallace T. Davis

Who is Volunteers of America?

Volunteers of America (VOA) was founded in 1896 by Christian social reformers Maud and Ballington Booth as a ministry of service to support America's most vulnerable population. Serving the entire United States, VOA is committed to helping those in need through our Christian faith-based roots in each community. The Southeast affiliate began in October 1980. Information about Volunteers of America can be found on our national website, www.voa.org, or on our local website, www.voase.org.

Volunteers of America's mission is that of reaching and uplifting all people and bringing them to the knowledge and active service of God. By illustrating the presence of God through all that we do, VOA serves people and communities in need and creates opportunities for people to experience the joy of serving others. Volunteers of America measures its success in the positive changes in the lives of individuals and in the communities we serve.

Uplifting Moments gives us an opportunity to share our values and faith and to offer a positive uplifting message. Proceeds from the sale of the book, *Uplifting Moments*, will benefit VOASE's programs and services. You can purchase the book at www.voase.org, by calling (251) 300-3500, or by visiting our corporate office at 1204 Hillcrest Road, Mobile, Alabama, 36695.

Visit our website, www.voase.org, to learn how you can become a part of the marvelous work of VOASE through your service or your financial investment.

There are no limits to caring®

There are no limits to caring® is a tag line, or registered statement, owned by Volunteers of America, Inc. and licensed for use to the local affiliates. We have used this tag line in many publications and statements.

In each radio and television spot we share, that's our message: *There are no limits to caring*®. But how is it lived out in the everyday world? What does this statement mean in the real world?

For the spouse who is abused, it may mean that he/she begins to care for self—and move out of a destructive relationship. That may be the first step to finding no limits to caring for self and others.

For the family of the alcoholic, it may mean to engage a professional interventionist to get the family member in treatment. And that is a tough decision on the family, but it is demonstrating… *There are no limits to caring*®.

For the adult child who won't accept responsibility, it may mean letting that person experience the challenges of life without a rescue attempt. It's called tough love. The only problem with tough love is that it is equally tough on the person who gives it. Tough love may be a part of this concept of no limits to caring.

And in our day-to-day lives, we can always find an opportunity to show to another human being that *There are no limits to caring*®. We use this tag line, not to promote guilt trips, but to encourage us to care for one another in our journey of life.

Suggestions on Using this Devotional Book

This devotional book is not written to be an intense Bible study but it is written in hopes that it can contribute to your relationship with God as you daily take time to pull away and listen to what God is saying to you right now. God is at work. (Romans 8:28) And we want to be a part of what He is doing. He will tell us if we but listen! Use your Bible. Search for additional scripture and spend time praying. The purpose of this book is to stimulate you in your relationship with God and one another.

1. Set aside definite time to read, pray, and meditate.
2. Read the scripture that is identified at the beginning of each day.
3. Give God time to speak to you from His Word.
4. Look for other scriptures that speak on this topic.
5. Read the uplifting moment. What is it saying to you, right now?
6. What can you gain to put to work this day? How can you serve others?
7. Prayer time. Talk with God as He is right in the room with you.
8. During the day, let this experience speak to you.
9. Share with someone what God has said to you on this day.

There are no limits to caring ®

There are no limits to caring ®

January 1

It is pleasant to see dreams come true (Proverbs 13:19, NLT).

Ranch

The son of a poor traveling horse trainer was asked to write a paper in senior high school. The subject "What do you want to do when you grow up?"

So he wrote of someday owning a ranch. He drew a diagram of a 200- acre ranch with a 4,000-square-foot house. When he got the paper back, there was a large F with a note that read, "See me after class."

The boy asked, "Why did I receive an F?'" The teacher responded, "This is an unrealistic dream for a boy like you. You have no money and come from a poor family. Owning a horse ranch requires a lot of money. There's no way you can do it."

Today, this former student now owns a 4,000 square-foot house in the middle of a 200-acre horse ranch.

Whether your dreams for this New Year are realistic or not, don't let anyone steal your dreams.

Happy New Year!

January 2

You are from God and have overcome them, for he who is in you is greater than he who is in the world (1 John 4:4, ESV).

Growth

In the 1920's, a British expedition attempting to climb Mt. Everest failed miserably after three attempts. An avalanche killed the leader and most of his party. Later, one of the survivors, with tears in his eyes, addressed the mountain.

He said, "Mount Everest, you defeated us once. You defeated us twice. You defeated us three times. But Mount Everest, we shall someday defeat you because you can't get any bigger, but we can."

As we face this New Year, some of our challenges may seem insurmountable. They may loom like mountains before us. But the truth is, we have the capacity to grow and change. We can keep coming back, and we can overcome obstacles if we are open to growth and change.

Some problems, like mountains, can be tough. But we can be tougher. Keep growing, and watch your obstacles get smaller.

January 3

I focus on this one thing: Forgetting the past and looking forward to what lies ahead (Philippians 3:13, NLT).

Look Ahead

2000 years ago, a young artist studied under a respected teacher. After several years, the student had learned to paint an exquisite work of art. He admired it so much that he spent days gazing at it.

One morning he arrived at his art studio and was shocked to find that his work of art was ruined…blotted out with paint. Angry, he ran to his teacher, who admitted to destroying the painting.

The teacher explained, "I did it for your own good. That painting was hindering your progress. Start again and see if you can do better."

The student took his teacher's advice and produced one of the finest paintings of antiquity.

Are you looking back at the previous year with satisfaction? Or are you looking back with regret? Whatever the case, this is a chance for a new start. Begin again, and you will find that you can do better.

January 4

Don't jump to conclusions—there may be a perfectly good explanation (Proverbs 25:8, MSG).

Small Town Justice

A police officer in a small town stopped a motorist who was speeding down Main Street. "But officer," the man said, "I can explain."

"Just be quiet!!!" snapped the officer, "…or I'll let you cool off in jail until the chief gets back."

"But officer, I just wanted to say…"

"And I said KEEP Quiet! Now you're going to jail!"

A few hours later, the officer checked up on his prisoner and said, "Lucky for you that the chief's at his daughter's wedding. He'll be in a good mood when he gets back." "Don't count on it," said the man. "I'm the groom!"

Wow…a lot of stress could be avoided if we could listen to each other…if a mother could listen to her daughter or a husband to his wife…or even a police officer, or a person in charge of the people we serve! God listens carefully to us; maybe we should go to one another.

There are no limits to caring ®

January 5

Put off your old self . . . an put on the new self, created after the likeness of God (Ephesians 4:22-23, ESV).

Conditioning

In India, when elephants are young, they have a rope tied around one of their legs and then attached to a wooden stake in the ground. This limits the distance they can go and keeps them safe, secure, and keeps them in place.

As these elephants get older, their minds become conditioned; they will still go only as far as the length of the rope. They do not realize that they now have the strength to pull the stake and walk away.

Many times, we act like those conditioned elephants. We become so conditioned to a situation; we feel stuck without realizing we hold the power to change.

Ask yourself, "What is keeping me from making the changes I need to make in my life?" And then make those changes. You have the strength to pull up the stake and change.

January 6

Keep on asking, and you will receive what you ask for. Keep on seeking, and you will find. Keep on knocking, and the door will be opened to you (Luke 11:9, NLT).

Searching for Gold

During the 1849 California gold rush, two brothers sold all they had and went looking for gold. With the little money they had, they bought supplies.

Soon they discovered a mine and proceeded to extract the gold ore from the mine. Everything was going well at first, but then something strange happened. The vein of gold ore disappeared!

They continued to pick away, but their efforts were unsuccessful. The brothers soon gave up and decided to return home. They sold the mine and their equipment for a few hundred dollars and left for home, empty-handed.

The man who bought the mine examined it carefully and decided to keep digging in the same spot where the brothers had left off. And three feet deeper, he struck gold!

With a little more persistence, the two brothers would have become millionaires. The gold is always deeper than you think. Persistence pays off. Don't give up.

January 7

Don't think about the past. I am creating something new (Isaiah 43:19, CEV).

If Only!

Have you ever said, "If only"
If only I had a new job…
If only I had a good wife…
If only I had a million dollars
If only this cancer had not reoccurred
If only I had not turned left on a red light
If only….

What do you do about the "If onlys…" in your life?
As long as we live in "If only…" we won't ever be anything but a dreamer…

Some things you can't change…move on from those things. Some things you can change…you don't have to be a victim, you can change your path…you can be a better husband….you can prepare yourself for the better job …If only says you can't do anything about it… but you can change some things about yourself. You can't change others or your past, but you can change your future.

That's why we do what we do at VOA.

January 8

We only have five loaves of bread and two fish (Matthew 14:17, NIV).

57 Cents

A young girl went to Sunday School, but the room was so small, there was no place for her. The pastor found her sobbing and took her in.

She later told her father she would save her money for a new building to hold more children. She saved her pennies. Soon after, the little girl took ill and died. Her father gave her savings—57 cents—to the pastor, telling him the story.

The pastor told the church trustees about the 57 cents. One of them thought some property on Broad Street would be a great place to start. The pastor made a deal with the landowner, paying 57 cents down with a balance of $10,000. Another generous person paid off the rest of the note.

Today on this lot in Philadelphia sits Temple Baptist Church. What can God do with your gift?

January 9

Whoever wants to be a leader among you must be your servant (Matthew 20:16, NLT).

Servant Leadership

While doing a routine vandalism report at an elementary school, a police officer was interrupted by a little girl about six years old who asked, "Are you a policeman?" "Yes," he answered as he wrote his report.

"My mother said if I ever needed help, I should ask the police. Is that right?" "Yes, that's right," the policeman told her. "Well then," she said, extending her foot toward the policeman, "would you please tie my shoe?"

That policeman knew the meaning of being a servant. He happily tied her shoe, and she went on her way.

Are you willing to kneel down to serve, even though you have power and authority? Perhaps more importantly, are you willing to serve with a good attitude?

Servant leadership really started about two thousand years ago, when Jesus said, "I came not to be served, but to serve."

The most powerful person is the one who will serve.

January 10

Never walk away from someone who deserves help; your hand is God's hand for that person (Proverbs 3:17, MSG).

Investments

Steve Ford, son of the late President Gerald Ford, shared a story about his father. When Gerald Ford was in high school, his principal gathered $100 for a scholarship and sent him to the university. Unfortunately, the principal didn't live long enough to see Gerald Ford become president. But Gerald Ford said, "Here I stand because one man invested $100 in my life."

Lt. Gen. Willie Williams, a three-star general and one of the highest-ranking officers in the US Marine Corps was the child of a single mother on welfare. He credited his success to good teachers who bankrolled his first semester in college.

What amazing stories! Is there a young person you could invest in? Your contribution may be the hand-up that would change their future. Has someone invested in you?

Don't miss the opportunity to be a blessing to someone today.

January 11

There is no fear in love, but perfect love casts out fear (1 John 4:18, ESV).

Unconditional Love

On January 11, 2009, Brit Humes conducted a final interview of the Bush administration. He interviewed George W. Bush and his father, George Bush Senior.

Brit Hume asked the former president what kind of advice he had given to his son, George W., during his presidency. The president interrupted and said, "I have many advisors, but every time I called my dad, I didn't need advice, I needed his unconditional love."

No matter what one's position in life is, whether it's the most powerful man in the world or an unknown person, one will always need the unconditional love of a father.

May every parent know that their child needs unconditional love. And may every child know that no matter how tough life gets, they can always go to their parents for unconditional love. If that's not the way it is, it's not too late to change.

January 12

So God created man in his own image, in the image of God he created him; male and female he created them (Genesis 1:27, ESV).

Inferiority

Eleanor Roosevelt said, "No one can make you feel inferior without your permission."

Whoever you are, don't give anyone permission to make you feel inferior or less than. You may not be as rich, as young, as wise, as smart, or as sophisticated as others, but those traits don't make you inferior. You are not. You were created by God, inferior to none of his creation.

Don't live a life of inferiority. Live a life of value. Act like you have values. Think like you have values. Because you do!

And if you should suffer from feelings of inferiority, one of the best ways to overcome a sense of inferiority is to reach out to those who feel inferior and help them see their value in their own life.

January 13

I tell you the truth, anyone who doesn't receive the Kingdom of God like a child will never enter it (Mark 10:15, NLT).

Children's Prayers

Dear God: Please send a new baby for Mommy. The new baby you sent last week cries too much.

Dear God: Who did you make smarter? Boys or girls? My sister and I want to know.

Dear God: How many angels are there in Heaven? I would like to be the first kid in my class to know the answer.

Dear God: Could you please give my brother some brains? So far, he doesn't have any.

Dear Lord: Thank you for the nice day today. You even fooled the TV weatherman.

Dear God: Please help me in school. I don't need help with anything else.

Dear God: Do you have any helpers in Heaven? I would like to be one of Your helpers in Heaven when I have summer vacation.

Dear God: I need a raise in my allowance. Could you have one of your angels tell my father?

The honesty of children is refreshing.

January 14

Truly I tell you, whatever you did for one of the least of these brothers and sisters of mine, you did for me
(Matthew 25:40, NIV).

Cheeseburger

John works with VOA Southeast in a tough neighborhood, reaching out to those who are underprivileged and exposed to difficult circumstances many others will never have to face.

One Sunday after church, John and his wife took some kids to McDonald's for lunch. He decided to order some extra cheeseburgers, take them back to the neighborhood, and pass them out. He came upon a group of guys relaxing on their porch. They received the cheeseburgers with smiles and hearty "Thank you's." One man, in particular, commented that he felt like Jesus had sent him that cheeseburger, and he decided that he would go to church that following Sunday.

Tragically, he was murdered three days later, shot ten times on the very porch where he ate that cheeseburger. We never know how important an act of kindness is.

For over a decade, John and Delores Eads have shared the love of Christ in an area filled with violence and crime. What started with a hamburger has blossomed into a ministry where Christ is exalted, friendships are made, and hope is provided. When we hear that still small voice urging us to do something for others, we either ignore or obey. Obey, be a blessing today.

January 15

Be kind and compassionate to one another (Ephesians 4:32, NIV).

Human Relations

John Maxwell suggests ten commandments of human relations:

(1) Speak to people. (2) Smile at people. (3) Call people by name. (4) Be friendly and helpful. (5) Be cordial. (6) Have a genuine interest in people. (7) Be generous with praise. (8) Be considerate of the feelings of others. (9) Be thoughtful of the opinions of others. (10) Be alert to give service.

If you practice implementing these commandments each day with each person you meet, specific results will occur. Your friends will multiply. Your reputation as a wonderful person will spread far and wide. And, your self-esteem will sky-rocket!

Each of us is capable of doing each one of the ten commandments of human relations. Meet people today with a desire to reach out to them in a positive, caring manner. The reward will be yours as you discover that there are no limits to caring.

January 16

Whatever you do, work at it with all your heart
(Colossians 3:23, NIV).

Try

Cecil Dowdy was a great left tackle for the University of Alabama around 1965. In those days, Bear Bryant liked the small, quick lineman instead of the great big linemen, like from Nebraska. So, in a game with Nebraska, their defensive lineman was whipping Cecil Dowdy.

Bear Bryant turned to the bench and said to Dowdy's substitute, "Can you go in there and block that guy that is whipping Cecil?" The reserve said, "Well, I can try, coach." And Bryant said, "Well, sit down, Cecil's trying."

In a later game with Nebraska on News Year Day 1966, Cecil gained national recognition in the 39-28 Orange Bowl victory over Nebraska when he dominated Nebraska All-American lineman Wally Barnes. In describing Dowdy in 1966, Coach Bear Bryant said Dowdy was "the finest blocking tackle we've ever coached."

It's not enough to try. Move from trying to becoming the best ever!! That's a winner!

January 17

Though one may be overpowered, two can defend themselves. A cord of three strands is not quickly broken (Ecclesiastes 4:12, NIV).

Change

John F. Kennedy said, "Change is the law of life." Martin Luther King, Jr. said, "Change does not roll in on the wheels of inevitability but comes through continuous struggle." Some changes are good...a new baby, new house, new school year, a new job. And change can be bad...loss of a job, loss of loved ones, a divorce.

The only way we overcome the trials of change or celebrate the joy of change is by uniting together, reaching out and helping our neighbors, and most importantly...having faith.

Persevere. Keep the faith. God will help us find ways to overcome the problems in our lives. He will enable us to adapt to any change. But we must come together and have faith.

Many times it only takes one person to make all the difference. Consider Abraham Lincoln, Martin Luther King, Jr., and Louise Braille. Let God use you to bring a blessing out of your tragedy!

There are no limits to caring ®

January 18

Look at the birds of the air; they do not sow or reap or store away in barns, and yet your heavenly Father feeds them. Are you not much more valuable than they?
(Matthew 6:26, NIV).

Sparrow Hymn

In the early 1900's, Civilla Martin and her husband were friends with the Doolittles, a married couple who both had physical disabilities. Mrs. Doolittle had been bedridden for 20 years, and Mr. Doolittle was in a wheelchair.

Yet despite their physical challenges, they were known for their joyfulness and their Christian lives. One afternoon, Civilla was visiting the Doolittle's, and she commented on their hopefulness and cheerful attitude. Mrs. Doolittle replied, "His eye is on the sparrow, and I know He watches me."

Civilla Martin went home and wrote lyrics to the hymn, "His Eye Is on the Sparrow," a song that has brought comfort to countless people.

What a model the Dolittles are to us. One, they found joy regardless of their circumstances. Two, they had a faith to carry them through all circumstances.

January 19

So, I do not run aimlessly; I do not box as one beating the air. But I discipline my body and keep it under control (1 Corinthians 9:26-27, ESV).

Jack LaLanne

Jack LaLanne lived to the ripe old age of 96. He was one of the first fitness gurus inspiring people to eat healthily and exercise.

LaLanne ate healthily and exercised every day of his life until he died of complications from pneumonia.

He said that fitness transformed his life as a teenager, and he was inspired to help others transform their lives as well.

He said it's never too late to start getting fit. At 43, he performed over 1,000 pushups in 23 minutes. At 60, he swam from Alcatraz Island to San Francisco – handcuffed, shackled, and towing a boat.

At 70, he performed a similar feat. He said age was just a number.

Don't make excuses for yourself. Transform your life today. Be physically fit. Be all that God wants you to be.

January 20

He will once again fill your mouth with laughter (Job 8:21, NLT).

Computers/Cars

Bill Gates and the president of General Motors have met for lunch, and Bill is going on and on about computer technology.

"If automotive technology had kept pace with computer technology over the past few decades, you would now be driving a V-32 instead of a V-8, and it would have a top speed of 10,000 miles per hour," says Gates. "Or, you could have an economy car that weighs 30 pounds and gets a thousand miles to a gallon of gas.

In either case, the sticker price of a new car would be less than $50. Why haven't you guys kept up?"

The president of GM smiles and says, "Because the federal government won't let us build cars that crash four times a day."

Did I hear you laughing? Laughter is a great way to begin your day!! A good laugh can rejuvenate us—prevent the crash. Find laughter today

January 21

Bear one anothers' burdens, and so fulfill the law of Christ (Galatians 6:2, ESV).

Miep Gies

A Dutch woman, Miep Gies (meep geese), died in January 2010 at 100 years old. She hid Anne Frank and her family in 1944 for two years during World War 2.

After Gies' apartment was raided by the German police, she gathered up Anne's diary and locked it in a drawer, hoping that Anne would be released after the war.

When Anne's father, the only survivor of the Frank family, was released, Gies gave him the diary, and he later published it.

Throughout her life, Gies worked diligently to promote tolerance. For her courage, she was given the title "Righteous Gentile" by the Israeli Holocaust museum.

But Gies ignored any praise for her courageous efforts and rejected being called a "Hero." She said it shouldn't be heroic to do your human duty of helping others.

There are no limits to caring ®

January 22

So here I am today, eighty-five years old! I am still as strong today as the day Moses sent me out (Joshua 14:10-11, NIV).

Wrinkles and No Teeth

A 7- year old boy was looking at his newborn baby sister. Quite confused, he looked at his grandmother and said, "Why is she old? She has wrinkles and no teeth!"

Being old may have nothing to do with wrinkles and no teeth. Life is not so much about how old you are and what's missing, but how young you live.

Being young and old certainly do have things in common. But our attitude toward life makes one old or young.

You can be <u>old</u> when you are 25, or you can be <u>young</u> when you are 75; it has everything to do with how you see life. How old would you be if you didn't know how old you are? That says a lot about how you see yourself and life.

Like mind over matter, if you don't mind, it doesn't matter how old you are – or how many wrinkles you have!

January 23

The testing of your faith produces perseverance (James 1:3, NIV).

Tests

A young boy was overheard praying this bedtime prayer: "Now I lay me down to rest, and hope to pass tomorrow's test. If I should die before I wake, that's one less test I have to take."

Sometimes we feel overwhelmed by the tests of life. Without the stress of the negative, we could never experience the joy of the positive. A car battery requires both a positive and a negative charge to operate properly. Without the presence of both, the battery is useless.

So, just as the young boy saw a positive side to a negative situation—we too can look for positives in our difficult circumstance. Enduring the "test" might offer gratification and satisfaction instead of failure and defeat. Even failing a test often ensures knowledge.

The test doesn't make you a different person; it merely reveals who you really are. Today you will be tested – how will you respond?

There are no limits to caring ®

January 24

Don't put it off; do it now! Don't rest until you do
(Proverbs 6:4, NLT).

Move

The great architect, Frank Lloyd Wright, received a phone call from a man who was living in a house he had designed. The caller complained, "I'm sitting here at my dining room table. There is a leak in the roof over my head, and it's dripping on me!"

The architect's response was quick and simple: "Move."

There is a time in life when we need to move and not just sit and complain about what's hitting us on the head.

A time to move from self-pity - to thanksgiving.
A time to move from hatred and bitterness - to love.
A time to move from talking - to doing.
A time to move from complaining - to making a difference.
A time to move from caring only about self - to caring about others.
A time to move toward someone who needs a friend - for there are no limits to caring.

January 25

Listen to advice and accept instruction, that you may gain wisdom in the future (Proverbs 19:20, ESV).

Doggone

Dog lovers, listen up! If a dog were the teacher...You would learn stuff like:

- When loved ones come home, always run to greet them.
- Never pass up the opportunity to go for joy rides. Let the wind blow in your face.
- Take naps. Stretch before rising.
- Run, romp and play daily.
- Avoid biting when a simple growl will do.
- When you are happy, dance around and wag your entire body.
- No matter how often you are scolded, don't buy into the guilt thing and pout...run right back and make friends.
- Delight in the simple joy of a long walk.
- Be loyal.
- Never pretend to be something you're not.
- And, if what you want lies buried, dig until you find it.

Now that's doggone good advice. If you're not too big, you can learn great lessons from a dog.

January 26

The angel of the LORD encamps around those who fear him, and he delivers them (Psalm 34:7, NIV).

Protection

Early Native Americans had a unique practice of training adolescent boys. On the night of a boy's thirteenth birthday, he was put to one final test.

On this night, he was blindfolded and taken several miles away, to the middle of a thick forest, to spend the entire night alone. When he took off the blindfold, he would find himself in this dense forest, alone and afraid!

Every time a twig snapped, he probably imagined a wild animal ready to pounce. After what seemed like an eternity, morning would come, and the first light would reveal an astonishing truth to that boy.

The first thing he saw would be the figure of a man standing just a few feet away, armed with a bow and arrow. This man was the boy's father and had been there all night, watching over his son.

That's our job as parents to protect and train. And to always be there. There are no limits to caring!

January 27

To answer before listening—that is folly and shame
(Proverbs 18:13, NIV).

Shingles

Bob walked into the doctor's office, and the receptionist asked him what he had. Bob said, "Shingles." So, she wrote down his name, address, medical insurance and told him to wait for the nurse.

Fifteen minutes later, a nurse's aide came out and asked Bob what he had. He said, "Shingles." She wrote down his height, weight, medical history and took him to an exam room.

Thirty minutes later, a nurse came in and asked Bob what he had. Bob said, "Shingles." So, the nurse gave Bob a blood test, a blood pressure test and told him to remove his clothes and wait for the doctor.

An hour later, the doctor came in, found Bob sitting naked, and asked Bob what he had.

Bob said, "Shingles." The doctor asked, "Where?" Bob said, "Outside on the truck. Where do you want me to unload them?"

Saying what you mean may get you the right treatment.

January 28

"How many times shall I forgive my brother or sister who sins against me? Up to seven times?" Jesus answered, "I tell you not seven times, but seventy-seven times"
(Matthew 18:21-22, NIV).

Sacrifice

In Ernest Gordon's book *Miracle on the River Kwai,* he writes about his experience as a prisoner of war in a Japanese camp.

One afternoon, a shovel went missing. The officer in charge demanded that the missing shovel be produced. Nobody came forward, so the officer got his gun and threatened to kill them all.

Then, one man stepped forward. The officer put away his gun, picked up a shovel, and beat the man to death. When it was over, the officers found that there had been a miscount…no shovel was missing.

An innocent man had died to save the others. When the survivors were rescued, they lined up in front of their captors, and instead of attacking them, they insisted: "No more hatred. No more killing. It's time for forgiveness."

Perhaps in each of our lives, it's a time to forgive, to love, and to care.

January 29

Whatever is true, whatever is right, whatever is pure, whatever is lovely, whatever is admirable—if anything is excellent or praiseworthy—think about such things (Philippians 4:8, NIV).

Appreciate the Small Things

A high school teacher lost her husband to a sudden heart attack. A week after his funeral, she returned to school and shared some insights with her students

She said, "Each of us is put here on earth to learn, share, love, appreciate and give of ourselves. None of us knows when this fantastic experience will end. Perhaps this is God's way of telling us that we must make the most of every single day."

She then said, "Make me a promise. On your way to and from school, find something beautiful and notice it. It can be anything. A tree, the way sunlight strikes something, a pleasant odor. Cherish the small beautiful things, for they are the stuff of life. Anything we take for granted can be taken away so quickly."

Good advice. There is much beauty in the world. Notice it. Cherish it. Make the most of today.

January 30

And we know that in all things God works for the good of those who love him, who have been called according to his purpose (Romans 8:28, NIV).

Proposal

Reed was excited about proposing to his girlfriend, Kaitlin. So he decided to put the ring in her milkshake, hoping to surprise her with an unforgettable proposal.

But he was so eager to have her find the ring that he challenged her to a race to see who could finish their milkshake first. She finished it but didn't find the ring.

As Kaitlin was racing to finish, she gulped the ring down without knowing. Horrified, Reed confessed that he had put her engagement ring in the milkshake.

Reed's proposal did not go according to plan. To celebrate their engagement, Reed took his fiancé to the hospital for x-rays. There they saw the truth, an image showing the engagement ring inside her. Doctors assured her that the ring would pass in a few days.

Sometimes life doesn't go according to our plan. Mistakes happen; things go wrong. But just remember the old adage, "This too shall pass."

January 31

Dear friends, never take revenge (Romans 12:19, NLT).

Peter the Great

Peter the Great, a czar of Russia, was interested in dentistry as a hobby and sometimes watched dentists as they practiced. One morning a friend asked Peter to help his wife. He explained that his wife was suffering from a severe toothache but refused to have the tooth pulled and even pretended to be in no pain.

Peter was happy to help, so he collected his dental instruments and followed the friend to his apartment. The man's wife protested and struggled, but Peter was able to extract the tooth successfully.

Later, Peter discovered that the wife, in fact, never had a toothache at all. The painful extraction had been her husband's revenge for an argument he had with his wife.

Fighting tooth and nail is not the way to handle arguments with your spouse. Revenge destroys. Don't take out your anger on one another. That's advice you can really sink your teeth into.

February 1

Anyone who loves God must also love their brothers and sisters (1 John 4:21, NIV).

Gift of Love

As a family finished dinner one evening, the five-year-old daughter wrote a note that said, "I love you!" She came around the table with a smile, showing each one her precious message.

Another four-old daughter didn't want to be left out and came around the table softly whispering to each member, "You are special."

The youngest, a three-year-old boy, decided he had to get in on the act too. In a not loud whisper, he told each family member, "You can have ice cream any time you want!"

All three children demonstrated love in their own special way.

What is your special way? A simple "I love you"? Or maybe a note expressing affection or appreciation. A phone call offering a word of encouragement. You get the idea. Love, which is "expressed," is really the only kind of love!

February 2

Whatever your hand finds to do, do it with all your might
(Ecclesiastes 9:10, NIV).

Marley and Me

The movie *Marley and Me* is based on a book written by John Grogan about his beloved dog, his family, and his life as a writer.

In the movie, John and his wife move to Florida. There he applies for a job as a reporter at a newspaper. While being interviewed for the job, the employer asks, "Why should I hire you?"

John's response was simple. He said, "I can surprise myself. I surprised myself by going to college and graduating with honors. I surprised myself by marrying the most wonderful woman. And if you hire me, I know I can surprise myself again, and I will surprise you too."

Many times, we lower our expectations of what we can do. Maybe we don't put 100 percent into something. It could be a job, a relationship, or even a chore. Give your all, be dedicated, and be committed. You may find that you surprise yourself and others.

February 3

And who knows but that you have come to your . . . position for such a time as this? (Ester 4:14, NIV).

George Lucas

George grew up in a small California town. As a teenager, he developed a passion for cars and drag racing. He wanted to become a professional racecar driver and spent a great deal of time and money on his car to make it suitable for racing.

Just days before his high school graduation, he was in a near-fatal car accident, which destroyed his car and sent him to the hospital for three months.

The accident shattered George's dream of pursuing a career as a professional racecar driver. Unsure of his future, he decided to enroll in college.

While attending college, he became interested in photography and quickly discovered a talent for filmmaking. Today George Lucas is known as the creator of some of the most popular films of all time, *Star Wars*.

Events can alter the course of our lives. But it's often in those difficult times that we discover who we really are.

February 4

What you have seen with your eyes do not bring hastily to court, for what will you do in the end if your neighbor puts you to shame? (Proverbs 25:7-8, NIV).

Judging Before the Facts

A lady returned to her car from shopping and found four men entering her vehicle. She drew a pistol from her purse and started screaming, "I have a gun, and I know how to use it! Get out of that car!"

The men ran like crazy. The lady, somewhat shaken, got into the car and tried to get her key in the ignition. The key wouldn't fit - she was in the wrong car! Later she found her own car.

She drove to the police station and reported her actions. The desk sergeant burst into laughter and pointed down the counter to four pale men who were reporting a carjacking by a crazy old woman who threatened them with a gun.

Sometimes we are so sure we're right that we'd kill! But just maybe, there's another way to see it. Perhaps we should be open-minded for the rest of the story.

February 5

Whoever serves me must follow me (John 12:26, NIV).

Lead by Following

A young woman who had her heart set on going to college was almost put off by a question on the application. The question was, "Are you a leader?" Attempting to be honest and conscientious, she wrote, "No." She fully expected to be rejected.

However, she received the following reply from the college: "Dear Applicant: A study of application forms reveals that this year our college with have 1,452 new leaders. We are accepting you because we feel it is imperative that they have at least one who follows!" Honesty can be refreshing, and it is also rewarding.

Where would leaders be without those who follow? One hit song said, "Life's a dance, we learn as we go, sometimes we lead, and sometimes we follow!" Knowing when to lead and when to follow is the trick, particularly in our educational funding crisis that demands leadership and followship. One thing is for sure, we always take the lead when we tell the truth.

February 6

And let us consider how we may spur one another on toward love and good deeds (Hebrews 10:24, NIV).

Encouragement VOSS

On this day in 2012, Janice Voss died. She was a brilliant astronaut who tied the record for the most space flights by a woman and developed experiments that were used on the International Space Station.

She documented her career as an astronaut, which had been a difficult and challenging career. She decided to donate her documentation of her career to the library at Purdue. She had always been encouraged to read the works of other astronauts before her and see their struggles and journey.

Knowing that someone else had overcome difficult times had inspired her to keep striving regardless of the challenges. And she, too, hoped that she might be an encouragement to others.

We each have people in our lives--- maybe your spouse or child --- who are watching our every step and listening to our words seeing how we handle difficulties. Are we setting an example of perseverance and encouragement regardless of circumstances?

February 7

If you help the poor, you are lending to the LORD--and he will repay you! (Proverbs 19:17, NLT).

La Guardia

La Guardia (la gwardia) served as mayor of New York in the 1930s. One time he decided to preside over Night Court, where a man was brought before him for stealing a loaf of bread, which he stole because his family was starving.

"I have to punish you," said La Guardia. "There are no exceptions to the law. I fine you ten dollars." As he said this, he reached into his own pocket and handed the money to the man. "Here's the ten dollars to pay your fine."

"Furthermore," he declared, "I'm going to fine everybody in this courtroom fifty cents for living in a city where a man has to steal bread to eat." The bailiff collected the fines and gave them to the man who left the courtroom with $47.

Every day we see people in our community who are in need... you'd be surprised what 50 cents a day can do for those in need in our community.

February 8

As each has received a gift, use it to serve one another, as good stewards of God's varied grace (1 Peter 4:10, ESV).

Get Lost

Anyone ever told you to "get lost?' Well, that's good advice!

No, not like it sounds, or like you might think. Like this: Gandhi said, "The best way to find yourself is to…lose yourself in the service of others." In other words, get lost! – In the service of others.

You may have time on your hands or be retired and feeling unfulfilled. Get Lost! Invest some time in meeting the needs of others, and you will find your best self. You will discover a satisfied and fulfilled YOU!

You may be feeling lonely or insecure. Get Lost! Find people who need your friendship. As you lose yourself in meeting their needs, you will find companionship and a sense of self-worth.

Getting lost…in serving others is good advice. You will really like the person you find in the mirror each day.

February 9

But now, Lord, what do I look for? My hope is in you
(Psalm 39:7, NIV).

Daffodils

We recently went to my parents' old home place and discovered the most beautiful little flower...the Daffodil ...bright yellow color on a small green stalk...everything else around it appeared dead...cold...hopeless...yet these were beautiful on this cold February day. We brought them home and planted them around our home.

Why would we do that? On a cold winter day, I want hope that spring is coming! After a cold, rough winter, one small plant gives forth a brilliant deep yellow color. It's not big, but it is beautiful.

That's what we are called to do...bloom in times of hopelessness. You may not be a big bloomer, but just bloom with a smile as radiant as a Daffodil, and others will see the hope that you have found during difficult times. My hope comes from my faith in God.

Bloom where you can use so that others can find faith, hope, and love!

February 10

Sluggards do not plow in season; so at harvest time they look but find nothing (Proverbs 20:4, NIV).

Bats in the Attic

While purchasing a home in New York, a couple found that a few bats were living in their attic. Not knowing how to get rid of them, they called an exterminator, who told them to wait a while before removing the bats because the babies were too young to fly.

Weeks rolled by as the couple got settled in their new home and soon forgot about the bats.

A few months later, they began to notice a foul odor. When they checked the attic, they were horrified to discover dead bats and 3,500 pounds of bat droppings in their attic. Hundreds of bats had been living in their attic, leaving behind piles of droppings.

Now, instead of removing a few bats, it will cost them $25,000 to clean up the mess.

It's easier to deal with a problem when it first begins. Don't let your problems pile up on you. If you procrastinate, you'll find that it creates a big mess.

February 11

Let us love one another, for love is from God (1 John 4:7, ESV).

Love Languages

Gary Chapman, in his book *The Five Love Languages*, explores how we communicate love. Love languages are:
1. Words of Affirmation
2. Quality Time
3. Receiving Gifts
4. Acts of Service
5. Physical Touch

Which is your love language? How do you express love, and how do you want love expressed to you?

Words of affirmation. We all need affirmation. However, some folks hear love through affirmation. It may be your spouse or child who needs words of affirmation from you.

Joan and Eddy had been married for 20 years. Their marriage was in trouble. No real communication. Then Joan discovered that her husband's love language was words of affirmation. Every day Joan would say words to affirm her husband. He found her love language was a need for physical touch. They learned the language of love – and freely gave it. What a difference it makes. Discover your love language.

February 12

Honesty guides good people (Proverbs 11:3, NLT).

Lincoln's Birthday

Today is the birthday of Abraham Lincoln. Raised in the backwoods of frontier America, he rose to be one of our nation's most outstanding leaders with less than one year of formal education.

Lincoln had a hunger and thirst for knowledge. Encouraged by his stepmother, he read the few books he could get his hands on. One of them was the Bible. Another was a biography of George Washington. Washington's life was most inspiring to Lincoln, and he determined to make Washington's ideals his own. That says a lot about role models and heroes. We tend to imitate those persons we admire.

Lincoln was also called "Honest Abe." He obtained that name the old-fashioned way – he earned it. Lincoln, like Washington, embraced honesty and integrity as a way of life, and our nation withstood a bloody civil war and remained a "United" States of America, largely because of his leadership.

February 13

By this all people will know that you are my disciples, if you have love for one another (John 13:35, ESV).

Valentine

Tomorrow is Valentine's Day. It's not too late to do something special for the love of your life. Valentine's Day is THE most popular time to express love and affection for our significant others.

But the truth is, every day provides an opportunity for us to express love and care to those close to us. We shouldn't wait for a special occasion to demonstrate to our loved ones how much we care for them. It doesn't have to be a box of chocolate or even a pretty card. Sometimes a simple, "I love you" spoken from the heart will do the job. Maybe just a hug and a word of appreciation, or a thoughtful gift, for no special reason other than to say, "I'm thinking of you." Expressions of love should be a daily exercise.

But tomorrow, do something extra special. It's Valentine's Day. How will you express your love?

February 14

[You] should always pray and never give up (Luke 18:1, NLT).

Hallmark

In the early 1900s, J.C. Hall was a young boy, working odd jobs to supplement his family's small income. Hall's father would always say, "The Lord will provide," to which Hall would respond, "It's a good idea to give the Lord a little help."

Hall excelled as a salesman. Others took notice and were impressed with his hard work. In 1908, he and his brothers bought picture postcards to sell.

Years later, Hall opened a store selling postcards. But then a fire destroyed the business. He was in debt, and it was the time of the Great Depression. Unwilling to give up, he opened a new shop and began making his own greeting cards. The cards were marketed under the name "Hallmark."

Today, millions of Hallmark greeting cards are sold each year. In fact, Hallmark makes their biggest profit on Valentines' Day. Persistence is a hallmark of success. Quitting is a hallmark of failure. Your choice.

February 15

Love your enemies, do good to those who hate you (Luke 6:27, ESV).

What Does Love Mean?

Ask yourself... "What does love mean?" A group of professionals posed this question to a group of 4 to 8 year-olds. A 6-year-old girl responded, "If you want to learn to love better, you should start with a friend you hate."

Wow! How do you define love? The Bible says, "Love is patient, love is kind, it does not envy, it does not boast, it is not proud, it does not dishonor others, it is not self-seeking, it is not easily angered, it keeps no record of wrongs. Love does not delight in evil but rejoices with the truth. It always protects, always trusts, always hopes, always perseveres."

Each day, through our regular routines, we can let our light shine, and those around us will be drawn to the love of God.

Pay attention to how you treat others. Today you may be the closest encounter that a person has with Jesus.

February 16

What has been will be again, what has been done will be done again; there is nothing new under the sun
(Ecclesiastes 1:9, NIV).

Something to Say

I believe it was Alfred North Whitehead who said, "Everything has been said before by someone." That's probably true. There is nothing new I can say…so why am I saying something that's already been said, something you have already heard?

The purpose is to give a positive voice in a negative climate…To remind you of the truths you already know…To encourage you to be your best…To enable us to see the difference we can make…To enable us to see possibilities not seen before…To provide a moment that might stimulate thinking.

Everything has been said before by someone. There's no original stuff – but who needs the original stuff – when you have love, kindness, and compassion. Those are things that we all need to receive and need to give every day. Just do what you already know – for there are no limits to caring.

February 17

Without wood a fire goes out; without gossip a quarrel dies down (Proverbs 26:20, NIV).

Gossip

Jennifer repeated a rumor about her neighbor. Soon, the entire community knew the gossip. The neighbor was deeply hurt. Jennifer was very sorry and went to a wise old man for advice on how to repair the damage.

"First, go to a chicken farm and get some chicken feathers," the wise man told her. "On your way home, drop them along the road, one by one." So, she did. The next day the wise man said, "Go and collect all those feathers you dropped yesterday." Jennifer searched for hours and returned with only three feathers.

The old man said, "It's easy to drop them, but it is impossible to get them back. So it is with gossip. Rumors are easy to spread. And once you do, you can never fully undo the wrong."

Say something positive about your neighbor, friend, or family. "You are a great friend," "You have a beautiful yard," "You are the best dad."

Those kinds of positive statements will change your world.

February 18

Do not forget to do good and to share with others, for with such sacrifices God is pleased (Hebrews 13:16, NIV).

Dale Earnhart

Dale Earnhardt, Sr., winner of seven Winston Cup championships, died while at the pinnacle of American motorsports. Earnhardt has been credited with taking Nascar racing to the heights of popularity that it enjoys today.

He was called "The Intimidator" because of his aggressive style of driving. He didn't mind "swapping paint" with his competitors out on the track. But he was also a man who gave back to the sport that had been so good to him. He was noted for his charity and benevolence off the track.

The last moments of his life were spent holding back from the lead, blocking other drivers. He wanted his son and Michael Waltrip, whom Earnhardt had sponsored, to vie for the lead. Waltrip, who had never won a major race, in fact, did win. No one would have been prouder than Dale Earnhardt, Sr.

February 19

A cheerful look brings joy to the heart (Proverbs 15:30, NLT).

Garbage Truck

Janet was going to the airport and hopped into a taxi. A few blocks down, traffic became heavy, and suddenly a car pulled out of a parking space right in front of the taxi.

The taxi driver slammed on his breaks, skidded, and missed the other car by just inches. The driver of the other car turned around and started yelling at the taxi. But the taxi driver just smiled and waved.

Janet asked the taxi driver, "Why are you so polite; after all, the other driver almost caused a horrible wreck?" The taxi driver explained, "Many people are like garbage trucks. They run around full of garbage: anger, frustration, and disappointment. As their garbage piles up, they need a place to dump it, and sometimes they dump it on people."

Don't take it personally. Just smile, wave, wish them well, and move on. Don't take on their garbage or spread it to other people.

There are no limits to caring ®

February 20

A friend is always loyal, and a brother is born to help in time of need (Proverbs 17:17, NLT).

Tim and Allison

Tim and his wife Allison were both fresh out of medical school and had been married for a few months. One morning Allison went for a bike ride when she crashed into a car. She was rushed to the hospital with severe injuries.

Her husband, Tim, was working in the emergency room when an unidentified woman arrived on a stretcher. He and his team began emergency treatment when suddenly he recognized the woman as his wife. With Tim's help, the nurses and physicians were able to save Allison's life. But weeks later, at home, an aneurysm in her head burst. Tim was there once again and saved her life until paramedics arrived.

Allison and Tim say that the experience brought them closer together, and they are a stronger team now. "I'll always be there for him, and he will always be there for me," says Allison.

Isn't that the way marriage works? Or even friendship? When trouble strikes, be a strong support to your loved ones.

There are no limits to caring ®

February 21

Let steadfastness have its full effect, that you may be perfect and complete, lacking in nothing (James 1:4, ESV).

Consistency

In high school, an instructor taught me to bowl. On the very first ball, I got a strike! I thought to myself, this is pretty easy, no big deal. But towards the end of the game, I realized that there was something very challenging - the challenge was to be consistent.

Consistency is very important, for instance, in family relationships. It creates healthy people. How we treat our spouse and children should be consistent from day to day. When we get a strike one time and a gutter ball the next, it causes those about us a great deal of confusion, not knowing what to expect from us.

Consistency creates an environment where people can depend upon who we are and what our values are.

Be consistent with who you are and your values, and do it every day. Just be consistent.

February 22

If you listen to constructive criticism, you will be at home among the wise (Proverbs 15:31, NLT).

Criticism/Anger

Joseph was a successful lawyer who had fled Hungary during the uprisings in 1956. When he arrived in the United States, he decided to use his knowledge of languages to get a job with an import-export company. He wrote a letter to the owner.

Weeks later, he received a reply from the company owner, who stated that they would not hire him because he could not write good English.

In his anger, Joseph wrote a rude reply to the owner. But he later tore the letter up. Maybe the man was right; after all, English wasn't his native tongue.

So Joseph wrote another letter to the owner, thanking him for pointing out his need for further study.

Two days later, he received a phone call inviting him for an interview. A week later, he went to work, where he later became the owner of the company.

How you handle criticism and anger will determine your success.

February 23

Know wisdom and instruction . . . understand words of insight (Proverbs 1:2, ESV).

Tid-bits of Wisdom

I'm constantly finding tid-bits of wisdom in my e-mail. Here's a sampling:
Following the path of least resistance is what makes rivers and men crooked.

To the world, you might be one person, but to one person, you might be the world.

Real friends are those who, when you feel you've made a fool of yourself, don't feel you've done a permanent job.

Sometimes the majority only means that all the fools are on the same side.

I don't have to attend every argument I'm invited to.

Life is 10% of what happens to you and 90% of how you respond to it.

Life is like an onion; you peel off one layer at a time, and sometimes you weep.

Each day is a gift from God! Don't forget to say, "Thank you!"

February 24

When I fall, I shall rise; when I sit in darkness, the LORD will be a light to me (Micah 7:6, ESV).

Dust Yourself Off

Kenny loved to get coffee at his favorite restaurant. Every day he would get a newspaper and sit down in his favorite spot, a booth by the window. He was sitting in that booth one evening when a minivan crashed through the wall and into his booth. The impact sent him flying across the room.

When the dust settled, Kenny calmly reached for his hat, put it on, got up, and began wiping off the dust and debris. He only had a few cuts and bruises, no serious injuries.

"It knocked the breath out of me, and I didn't realize at first what had happened," Kenny told reporters.

Can you believe, a few days later, Kenny was back at the restaurant enjoying a cup of coffee?

When life knocks the wind out of you, you have to get back up and dust yourself off. Don't be defeated by the interruptions in your life.

February 25

I will not violate my covenant or alter the word that went forth from my lips (Psalm 89:34, ESV).

Neil Armstrong

When Neil Armstrong walked on the moon, his first words were, "That's one small step for man, one giant leap for mankind." But just before he reentered the shuttle, he remarked, "Good luck, Mr. Gorsky."

NASA was puzzled about the statement since there was no Mr. Gorsky in the space program. Over the years, many people asked Armstrong about that statement, but he would just smile. But in 1995, after making a speech, a reporter asked Armstrong about the statement, "Good luck, Mr. Gorsky."

Armstrong finally responded. When he was a child, Mr. Gorsky was his neighbor. While playing outside, Armstrong heard his neighbors, Mr. and Mrs. Gorsky, arguing. He heard Mrs. Gorsky shout at Mr. Gorsky, "Sex! You want sex? You'll get sex when the kid next door walks on the moon!"

Promises are meant to be kept even if you have to walk on the moon. Don't forget your commitments to your family and friends. Keeping promises is love in deed.

February 26

By this we know love, that he laid down his life for us, and we ought to lay down our lives for the brothers (1 John 3:16, ESV).

Transfusion

A little girl suffered from a rare disease.

She was hospitalized, and her only chance of recovery was a blood transfusion from her 5-year-old brother. He had miraculously survived the same disease and developed antibodies needed to combat the illness.

The doctor explained the situation to the brother and asked if he would give his sister his blood. After a moment of hesitation, he said, "yes, I'll do it if it will save her."

As the transfusion progressed, he lay in bed next to his sister smiling as the color returned to her cheeks. Then his face grew pale, and he asked the doctor in a trembling voice, "Will I start to die right away?"

Being young, the little boy had misunderstood the doctor and thought he was going to have to give all his blood, his life, to his sister in order to save her.

We have a greater capacity to give than we realize if we only would just do it.

February 27

No discipline is enjoyable while it is happening—it's painful! But afterward there will be a peaceful harvest of right living for those who are trained in this way (Hebrews 12:11, NLT).

Leaving the Nest

When a mother eagle builds her nest, she starts with thorns, broken branches, sharp rocks, and many other items that seem entirely inappropriate for a nest.

But then she lines the nest with a thick padding of wool, feathers, and fur, making it soft and comfortable for the eggs. By the time the growing birds reach flying age, the comfort of the nest and the luxury of free meals make them reluctant to leave.

That's when the mother eagle begins "stirring up the nest." With her talons, she pulls up the thick lining of fur and feathers, bringing the sharp rocks and branches to the surface.

As more of the bedding gets plucked up, the nest becomes more uncomfortable for the young eagles. Eventually, the growing eagles are convinced to leave their once-comfortable nest and grow into mature adult eagles. As parents, we sometimes have to stir up the nest so that our children can mature and leave. Without this tough love, they will never grow up.

February 28

Whoever would be great among you must be your servant
(Matthew 20:26, ESV).

Responsibility

Over 40 years ago, I transported an 8-year-old boy who had been hit by a car while riding his bicycle to the hospital. I drove 12 miles, speeding, to save his life. When I arrived at the hospital and asked someone for a stretcher to take him in, I was told, "That's not my responsibility." The boy was in a coma for months, had life-long physical disabilities, but he did live.

I remembered that event as I drove to the door of the same hospital helping my weak, 86-year-old dad to the emergency room. A lady came out and asked if we needed a wheelchair. She brought the wheelchair and then pushed my dad into the building.

That wasn't her responsibility! But her focus was, "How can I help?"

As I glanced at her name tag, it read Chief Executive Officer. Servant leadership always gets the job done regardless of our title.

March 1

Your giving may be in secret. And your Father who sees in secret will reward you (Matthew 6:4, ESV).

Flower

A friend said, "I was several miles in deep forest when I came upon the most gorgeous flower I had ever seen. The flower was standing beautifully even though no one would ever see, admire or appreciate it.

It did what it was supposed to do because that's what it was, not because of reward or recognition."

You know that is the definition of character – it's who you are deep in the forest when no one sees you. Many people in our community do beautiful deeds that no one really notices.

That's what makes our community so wonderful – people doing what's beautiful with no expectation of recognition. Be beautiful and authentic wherever you are.

March 2

This is the kind of fasting I want . . . share your food with the hungry, and give shelter to the homeless. Give clothes to those who need them, and do not hide from relatives who need your help (Isaiah 58:7, NLT).

Lent

Ash Wednesday is the beginning of Lent. Lent is the forty-day season of fasting and prayer before the resurrection of Jesus. What will you give up for Lent? I heard about one guy who offered to give up his wife, but he quickly changed his mind! I heard one teenager offered to give up green beans. Of course, he didn't like green beans anyway!

We can be flippant or be serious about Lent. Lent was intended to be a time of serious reflection on our lives in preparation for Easter. Reflecting is a good idea, as our lives can get filled with unimportant things.

Our lives can get cluttered up with non-essentials. What could we give up that would give us more time to devote to real priorities such as - time with God, family, and friends, or volunteering to help people in need? A move in that direction is good, not only for Lent but for a lifetime.

March 3

That which was from the beginning, which we have heard, which we have seen with our eyes, which we looked upon and have touched with our hands, concerning the word of life— the life was made manifest. We have seen it, and testify to it and proclaim to you the eternal life, which was with the Father and was made manifest to us (1 John 1:102, ESV).

Wonders

As a middle school class studied the Seven Wonders of the Ancient World, the students were asked to list today's Seven Wonders. Receiving the most votes were:

Egypt's Great Pyramid, Taj Mahal, Grand Canyon, Panama Canal, Empire State Building, St. Peter's Basilica, and China's Great Wall.

While collecting the votes, the teacher noticed one student holding onto her paper, and she asked what the problem was. The girl answered, "There are so many wonders."

"I think the Seven Wonders of the World are to touch, to taste, to see, to hear, to feel, to laugh, and to love."

The silence in the room was deafening! It is far too easy for us to look at human achievements and refer to them as "wonders" while overlooking all the wonders God has given to each of us every day.

March 4

Encourage the fainthearted, help the weak, be patient with them all (1 Thessalonians 5:14).

Frogs

A group of frogs was traveling together when two of them fell into a deep pit. Observing the depth of the hole, the group shouted, "You will never be able to get out of that pit."

The two down in the pit started jumping. The other frogs kept shouting to them they were as good as dead and should quit trying. Finally, one frog became so exhausted, he just quit and died. The other frog continued to jump as hard as he could. Once again, the crowd at the top yelled for him to give it up.

The remaining frog started jumping harder and finally jumped out of the pit. The other frogs asked him why he kept trying. Didn't he hear them telling him to quit? He said, "I'm hard of hearing; I thought you were encouraging me to keep trying!"

Encouragement is a powerful tool! Help someone jump to new heights today by offering encouragement.

There are no limits to caring ®

March 5

The beloved of the LORD dwells in safety (Deuteronomy 33:12, ESV).

Hawks

At our home birds like to eat from our bird feeders. It's like a buffet, eat all you want and stay as long as you like!

Well, not always. Occasionally the birds don't come. But usually, we can look around and see a hawk flying overhead or sitting in a tree nearby. Hawks love to eat birds.

Hawks have a vision that is eight times better than humans. The hawks can quickly zoom down at speeds of 150 miles per hour, snatching up a bird…and have a great lunch. But when the birds see the hawks, they don't come out… they go to a safe place.

Wouldn't it be wonderful if our kids could learn when hawks are around… go home…find a safe place?

But then again, home for some is where the hawk lives. We all need a safe place to be, no matter our age. What hawk do you see?

March 6

As he thinks in his heart, so is he (Proverbs 23:7, NKJV).

Emperor Norton

Have you ever heard of Emperor Norton? His official title was "Emperor of the United States and Protector of Mexico." He brought a lot of joy and entertainment to the people of San Francisco from 1857 to 1880.

He was not a real emperor, just a happy man who had been a merchant and lost his fortune. He refused to let poverty defeat him, so he dressed himself like an emperor and paraded around the streets of San Francisco, spreading smiles and good cheer.

People started treating him like royalty even though he had nothing. He was treated to front row seats at theaters. Tailors designed and presented him with his royal uniforms at no cost. Railroads afforded him free transportation, and he was given an honorary seat in the state government. He was a prime example of what a great attitude can accomplish.

Control your attitude, or it controls you.

March 7

There is no longer Jew or Gentile, slave or free, male and female. For you are all one in Christ Jesus (Galatians 3:28, NLT).

Golf

In Scotland, a new game was invented. It was entitled Gentlemen Only Ladies Forbidden… GOLF and thus the word GOLF entered into the English language. No such thing now, it's not a men's only thing.

Throughout history, there have been times when we have forbidden people from participating in certain activities because of disability, race, or faith. In our community, no one must be prohibited from participating because of artificial barriers.

The truth of the matter is, everyone is beautiful in his/her own way. Each one should be free to achieve his/her own dreams.

Just think, we have come a long way—women are now playing golf, no longer forbidden.

Don't let anyone forbid you from achieving your dreams just because you are of a different gender, race, or have something physical that's different. Forbid yourself from being placed in a box that keeps you from experiencing all of life.

March 8

Everyone should be quick to listen, slow to speak and slow to become angry (James 1:19, NIV).

Healing for Hearing

In a church one Sunday morning, a preacher said to the congregation, "Anyone with special needs who wants to be prayed over, please come forward to the front by the altar.

With that, Leroy got in line, and when it was his turn, the preacher looked at him and asked, "Leroy, what do you want me to pray about for you?" Leroy replied, "Preacher, I need you to pray for help with my hearing."

The preacher put one finger of one hand in Leroy's ear, placed his other hand on top of Leroy's head, and then began to pray. He prayed with such enthusiasm that the whole congregation joined in prayer for Leroy.

After a few minutes of praying, the preacher removed his hands, stood back, and asked, "Leroy, how is your hearing now?" Leroy answered, "I don't know. I'll find out at the courthouse next Tuesday afternoon."

Communication even to people we really like is challenging! How is your hearing?

March 9

You have shown me great kindness (Genesis 19:19, ESV).

Good Ole Boy

He was just a good ole boy, never meaning no harm…didn't like to pick up after himself and certainly didn't like to clean the house. But one day, he decided that he would surprise his wife…he would clean the house. And he did. He cleaned it from one end to the other. And it was spotless.

When the wife got home from work, she couldn't believe her eyes. She thought, "What has this guy done? He must be trying to amend for his ways!" And she became very concerned about what she did not know.

And when she tried to find out what she did not know, she soon realized that she did know everything. The good ole boy was just trying to do something nice for his wife – and she couldn't believe it.

Sometimes even the good ole boys can do something really outstanding. And maybe we should simply accept it, not try to analyze it or discount it, but just enjoy the moment.

Believe the best in your spouse, and you will see miracles.

March 10

Do to others as you would like them to do to you (Luke 6:31, NLT).

Sweet Spouse

In the early years of their marriage, Prince Philip and Princess Elizabeth traveled to Vancouver Island on a Canadian destroyer. The waters were very turbulent, tossing the ship about.

A young petty officer was assigned to deliver a large tray of cakes for the Prince and Princess to their royal suite. As he entered the suite, the ship lurched wildly, and he accidentally spilled the cakes on the floor.

To his amazement, Prince Philip immediately got on his hands and knees and crawled around, gathering several cakes before returning to his chair. The Prince sat down and turned to his wife, Princess Elizabeth. Smiling, he said, "I've got mine. Yours are down there."

Turbulent waters as we live in today may toss you about. But a marriage works best when you think of your spouse before yourself.

No one said marriage is a piece of cake but take time today to do something sweet for your spouse.

March 11

Commit to the LORD whatever you do, and he will establish your plans (Proverbs 16:3, NIV).

Jim Morris

Jim's childhood dream was to become a major league baseball player. He made it to the minor leagues but retired because of several injuries. He abandoned his dream and became a high school baseball coach.

As a coach, Jim worked to inspire his team to have goals and pursue their dreams. But his team challenged him to pursue his dream of playing in the major leagues.

His team cut a deal: if they won District Championship, Jim would try out for the major leagues. Jim's team indeed won the District Championship. Jim did try out, and he threw pitches at ninety-eight miles per hour.

Three months later, he achieved his dream of pitching in the major leagues. At thirty-five years old, Jim Morris became the oldest rookie to play in major league baseball despite all odds.

What are your dreams? Your goals? No matter how old we become or where life takes us, dreams are never out of reach.

March 12

Encourage one another and build one another up (1 Thessalonians 5:11, ESV).

One Another

How we treat one another at home, work, or anywhere is very important. An ancient book offers wisdom regarding the way we should treat one another. It says, Love one another. Be kind to one another. Honor one another. Encourage one another. Comfort one another. Serve one another. Submit to one another. Be patient with one another. Forgive one another. Pray for one another. Of course, those words are from the Bible.

The movie *Radio* tells the story of how a football coach treated an intellectually challenged man with dignity and respect. He helped a town understand that treating other people with compassion and care is more important than a winning football season. Life is more than winning games; it's all about relationships.

While we live in a culture that magnifies individual achievement at the expense of relationships, our greatest successes will be seen in how we treat one another.

March 13

Put on then, as God's chosen ones, holy and beloved, compassionate hearts (Colossians 3:12, ESV).

Learning Compassion

At what age do you learn compassion? It may be younger than you think. A six-year boy saved his allowance for six weeks. On the next Sunday, he presented the money, $5, to his preacher. The preacher asked, "Why are you giving me $5?" "I just want to help you, 'cause Daddy said you were the poorest preacher we have ever had."

Well, there could have been a communication problem there, but at least the dad had taught his son compassion at an early age. So did mine.

Parents have the opportunity to teach compassion to children both in word and deed. Compassion is something children need to hear and see demonstrated each day.

What if we lived in a country where children knew more about compassion than violence, more about giving than taking?

What do we teach our children? Compassion for others. How to give. How to care.

Now that's the lesson that we all need to learn at an early age.

March 14

Show me the right path, O LORD; point out the road for me to follow (Psalm 25:4, NLT).

Einstein

Years ago, Albert Einstein was on a train to New York. As the ticket taker approached, Einstein couldn't find his ticket. He began frantically searching his pockets, turning them inside out, but still could not produce the ticket.

The ticket taker said, "Don't worry, Mr. Einstein. Forget about it." Twenty minutes later, the ticket taker came back through the car and saw Einstein on the floor searching everywhere for his lost ticket.

Again the ticket taker tried to reassure Einstein by saying, "I told you not to worry about the lost ticket. We trust that you purchased one."

Einstein looked up at the railroad employee and said, "Young man, this isn't a matter of trust but of direction. I need to find the ticket because I forgot where I am going."

Have you lost your direction? If you got where you are going, where would you be? If you know where you're going, you'll know when you arrive.

There are no limits to caring ®

March 15

Defend the weak and the fatherless; uphold the cause of the poor and the oppressed. Rescue the weak and the needy (Psalm 82:3-4, NIV).

Hope Springs Eternal

Many people in our community live from day to day without hope for a better life. Whether it be due to poverty or some disability, they see no real solution to their present circumstances.

As we move from the bleak, gray days of winter to the greening of spring, nature offers a lesson. Green leaves and blossoms will soon replace that which appeared to be dead and lifeless. Springtime brings a message of hope. Spring reminds us that life is always present, even when it seems hopeless.

At VOA, we seek to provide solutions for those who have no hope or who have lost hope. You can be a part of that effort by reaching out to someone today who needs a helping, caring hand. Contact us today – you can be a part of our mission – reaching and uplifting. Turn winter into spring. Show you care to someone who thinks no one cares.

March 16

He's famous for great and unexpected acts: there's no end to his surprises (Job 5:9, MSG).

Alfie

3 year-old Alfie was attending his first day of preschool. And he was not too happy about it. So he hatched a plan to escape. He stealthily snuck out of the building, climbed over a 3-foot wall, crossed a busy street, and walked home.

Alfie knocked on the door to his house, and his mother answered, shocked and hysterical to see her 3-year-old son standing there.

She called the school and discovered that they didn't even know Alfie had been missing.

Although his mother was upset with the school, she is thankful she was home when her son arrived.

Life always offers us surprises. Surprises on the other side of the door. Maybe things didn't go the way we planned. But count your blessings and focus on the positive.

March 17

Show kindness and mercy to one another (Zechariah 7:9, NIV).

Simple Kindness

Margie felt upset when she saw the same homeless person every time she went to the grocery store. Margie had to confront her own feelings. She looked the homeless person in the eye, smiled, and spoke to her. One day she introduced herself and learned the homeless lady's name. In the future, she would stop and chat. In those conversations, she learned of the traumatic experiences that had contributed to her condition of homelessness.

One day, she said to Margie, "It's people like you, people who see me as a person, that gives me the strength to keep trying. Last year, I didn't have anything to be thankful for. But this year, I thank God for you."

A simple act of kindness like a smile, a brief conversation, just recognizing another as a human being worth speaking to can make a radical difference in a person's life. Each of us will meet someone today who needs simple kindness.

March 18

I will forgive their wickedness and remember their sins no more (Hebrews 8:12, NIV).

Moody

The well-known evangelist Dwight L. Moody once visited a prison to preach to the inmates. After he had finished speaking, Moody visited a number of prisoners in their cells, asking each why he was there.

Again and again, inmates told him: "I shouldn't be here... I'm innocent... I was falsely accused..." Not one admitted that he was guilty.

At last, Moody found a man holding his face in his hands and weeping. The prisoner told Moody, "My sins are more than I can bear." Moody was so relieved to find an honest man that he unthinkingly exclaimed: "Thank God for that!" He then quickly explained that his remorse was sufficient for God's forgiveness.

You can never be free from your guilt without acknowledging your wrongdoing. If you are heavy with guilt, make it right. Find God's forgiveness. There may be someone in your life today who needs to hear you say, "Please forgive me."

March 19

Awake, awake, put on strength, O arm of the LORD, awake, as in days of old (Isaiah 51:9, ESV).

Wake

Back in the old days, lead cups were used to drink ale or whiskey. The combination would sometimes knock folks out for a couple of days. Someone walking along the road would take them for dead and prepare them for burial.

They would be laid out on the kitchen table, and the family would gather around, eat, drink, and wait to see if the person would wake up. Hence, the custom of holding a "wake."

We still live in a time when we are waiting to see who is going to wake up. Will it be those who are opposed to paying adequate dollars for education? Will it be those who have been written off as the lost generation? Maybe it is simply the family—is it dead or alive?

Perhaps in place of just hanging around—having a party, we can reach out in compassion to those who are struggling to wake up.

March 20

I will praise You, for I am fearfully and wonderfully made (Psalm 139:14, NKJV).

Freckles/Wrinkles

An elderly grandmother and her little grandson, whose face was sprinkled with bright freckles, spent the day at the zoo.

Many children were waiting in line to get their cheeks painted by an artist who was decorating them with tiger paws.

But a little girl in line behind the young boy said, "You've got so many freckles, there's no place to paint!"

Embarrassed, the little boy dropped his head. His grandmother knelt down next to him. "I love your freckles. When I was a little girl, I always wanted freckles," she said while tracing her finger across the child's cheek. "Freckles are beautiful." The boy looked up, "Really?" "Of course," said the grandmother.

"Why, just name me one thing that's prettier than freckles." The little boy thought for a moment, peered intensely into his grandma's face, and softly whispered, "Wrinkles."

Grandmothers and grandsons have their own unique beauty. So, do you.

There are no limits to caring ®

March 21

Can the Ethiopian change his skin or the leopard his spots? Then also you can do good who are accustomed to do evil (Jeremiah 13:23, ESV).

Weather Change

Our weather this past winter and early spring has been absolutely beautiful. God has outdone himself. Weather is something we can't change. We simply react to the weather, but there are things we can be proactive about. I've found it better to be proactive than reactive.

We can be proactive in taking the initiative to show kindness and love to people. We can be proactive in solving difficult problems confronting our community. When it comes to the weather, we can't do much to change it, but there are issues in life we can change. And we must be more than a thermometer.

God grant me the serenity to accept the things I cannot change, the courage to change the things I can, and the wisdom to know the difference. What a prayer!

March 22

God loves a cheerful giver (2 Corinthians 9:7, ESV).

Oseola

Oseola McCarty was a grammar school dropout, but she managed to save $150,000 by doing laundry and ironing. She gave all of her savings to create a scholarship fund at the University of Southern Mississippi. She said, "I can't do everything, but I can do something to help somebody. And what I can do, I will do."

When the story of her gift made the news, more than six hundred other donors added over $330,000 to the original scholarship fund. Ted Turner, the founder of CNN, was inspired to donate a billion dollars to the UN Health and Population programs. He said, "If that little woman can give away everything she has, then I can give a billion!"

Oseola McCarty's gift was inspiring and infectious. She demonstrated there are no limits to caring. Just imagine what YOUR gift might do!

There are no limits to caring ®

March 23

Out of . . . the perfection of beauty, God shines forth
(Psalm 50:2, ESV).

Spring

Spring is here... a message of hope. Spring reminds us that life is always present, even when it appears otherwise. God has created beauty for us to enjoy!

But sometimes, we fail to see the beauty. In our own minds, we may have a storm raging or a conflict or a fear that keeps us from seeing the beauty God has created...stress at work or home. Let it go. Maybe you have a conflict. Let it go. You need to forgive someone. Forgive and let it go. Perhaps you have a fear. Let it go and place your faith in God.

We have such a beautiful world to live in, but the world that we really live in is what we experience in our own minds. Today is a great day just to stop, relax, and let God speak to you through his beauty.

March 24

Call out for insight and raise your voice for understanding (Proverbs 2:3, ESV).

Puppies

A man was putting up a sign advertising puppies for sale when a little boy approached and asked if he could see them. The man whistled, and from the doghouse came Dolly, followed by four little balls of fur. The boy was delighted and pressed his face against the chain-link fence. He then noticed something stirring inside the doghouse. Slowly another puppy appeared. It was much smaller and very awkward.

The little boy said, "I want that one." The man knelt by the boy and said, "Son, you don't want that one. He will never be able to run and play like those others."

With that, the boy pulled up one of his pants legs, revealing a steel brace. He said, "I don't run too well myself, and this little fellow needs someone who understands."

Whether it is puppies or people, we all need someone who understands. Make a difference today by reaching out with understanding.

March 25

Therefore do not be anxious (Matthew 6:31, ESV).

Surprise Circumstance: Little Things

In Wisconsin, the power was suddenly knocked out for hundreds of customers. Rodney Johnson was stuck on an elevator at work when the power went out. He was trapped in the elevator for an hour and began to wonder if he would make it out alive.

Once a firefighter opened the door, Mr. Johnson wasted no time in getting out. "I'm surprised I didn't knock the fireman down," he said.

So, what caused this power outage? Two unfortunate squirrels. The squirrels came in contact with a transformer, which caused the outage. It turns out that these small creatures are one of the leading causes of power outages.

Even the smallest things can interrupt life, causing us to lose our tempers or even become depressed. But it's how we react to those surprise circumstances that make the difference. Because often, the problem is not as big as we think.

March 26

By this all people will know that you are my disciples, if you have love for one another (John 13:35, ESV).

Austin

In some ways, Austin is not a typical young boy. At the age of four, he starting saving his allowance so that each week he could buy food for the homeless. Austin says that feeding the homeless is the highlight of his life.

Wow! It wasn't his brother Lamical's fame as star running back for the Florida Gators that was the root of his compassion but instead his other brother Taylor who has autism. Austin's father says that he's always been a nurturer of his brother.

Before kids graduate from kindergarten, they are learning compassion and kindness. With each chicken sandwich, Austin hands out a message, "Don't forget to show love!"

We, too, can remember to "show love" each day as we bump into contact with other people who need your love, show compassion, respect… if a four-year-old can do it for the homeless… we can do it!

March 27

You, my brothers and sisters, were called to be free
(Galatians 5:13, NIV).

Josh Home

It seems like yesterday my son arrived home from Iraq. For over a year, he was separated from his family, friends, and the American way of life we sometimes tend to take for granted. While he was gone, his wife gave birth to a beautiful son. Josh missed a year of his son's life.

What is the cost of not being with your son during his first year? Yet all of our military families pay a similar price for serving our county...all of those days and nights without a spouse to give a helping hand... It's a high price so we can enjoy our freedom.

My son received the bronze star. He made his family proud and served his country well. What more could you ask?

Freedom is not free, and each day thousands are paying the price to protect us from those who would destroy our way of life. Give thanks to this great country and those who serve.

March 28

This service that you perform is not only supplying the needs of the Lord's people but is also overflowing in many expressions of thanks to God (2 Corinthians 9:12, NIV).

Fred

Fred Factor is a book about Fred, a mailman who loves what he does. He is an average-looking man; nothing about his appearance would convey anything out of the ordinary. But his sincerity and warmth are definitely extraordinary. He cares about people.

When Mr. Sanborn first met him, Fred was eager to know how he could better deliver his mail.

Mr. Sanborn travels frequently, and Fred would make special arrangements to deliver the mail when Mr. Sanborn was out of town, even watching over the house.

Where others might see delivering the mail as tedious work, Fred sees an opportunity to serve… to do more than is required.

Fred's spirit of service led Mr. Sanborn to create the Fred Award to present to his employees who demonstrated that same spirit of service and attitude.

You can be a Fred, no matter what your job is; wherever you are and whatever you do, you can serve others.

There are no limits to caring ®

March 29

Fear not, for I am with you (Isaiah 41:10, ESV).

Overcoming Fear

The words "fear not" are in the Bible hundreds of times. God did not design us to live a life overcome with fear. In 1 John 4:18, the Bible says that perfect love casts out fear.

God is perfect love, and through Him, we can overcome fear which can include anxiety, depression, and many other things.

In order to let God's perfect love be bigger than our fears, we must first realize how much He loves us. Next time you feel fear creep into your life, take a second to reflect on God's love for you and for others.

If God opens a door for you, walk through it with the comfort of knowing that He will give you what you need to accomplish, what He has set out for you to do.

We are given many moments each day to overcome fear and walk in God's love. Rest in Him, and fear will no longer be a driving force in your life.

March 30

You'll do best by filling your minds and meditating on things true, noble, reputable . . . the best, not the worst (Philippians 4:8, MSG).

Believe the Best

Phil Esposito played for the North America ice hockey league during the early 1970s. During the time of the Cold War, his team went to Moscow to play the Soviet team. The hockey league was suspicious that the hotel rooms had been bugged. So Esposito and several others searched the hotel room for microphones.

After searching diligently, they found a strange-looking, round piece of metal embedded in the floor in the center of the room, under a rug.

They were sure they had found a hidden microphone, so they began to dig it out of the floor. Suddenly the piece of metal came loose, and that's when they heard a crash beneath them.

They had released the anchor to the chandelier in the ceiling below.

Believing the worst in others can sometimes bring the roof down on you. Believe the best, or if you go looking for trouble, it will find you.

March 31

A glad heart makes a cheerful face (Proverbs 15:13, ESV).

Benefits of Laughter

Have you ever paid attention to how good you feel after a good laugh? Enjoying a funny video of a pet playing around, watching a child experience something funny for the first time, or laughing at something silly we or someone else has done.

Research shows that laughter causes your blood vessels to dilate by 22 percent, which helps improve blood flow and, in turn, lowers blood pressure. Studies also demonstrate that laughter elevates your mood, raises energy levels, reduces pain and stress, and the list goes on and on.

God never ceases to amaze, even in the little things. He created laughter and designed it in such a way that it provides our bodies with numerous health benefits. What a great God He is!

Laughter is the best medicine, and it's free! Surround yourself with positive people that will bring joy and laughter into your life and laugh!

April 1

Whoever guards his mouth and tongue keeps his soul from troubles (Proverbs 21:23, NKJV).

Preacher's Joke

A pastor attended a minister's conference. One speaker approached the podium and said, "The best years of my life were spent in the arms of a woman that wasn't my wife!"

Mouths dropped open in shock until the speaker quickly replied, "And that woman was my mother!" Everyone burst into laughter, and the speaker delivered the rest of his talk, which went very well.

The next Sunday, the pastor decided to incorporate that joke into his sermon. But the joke now seemed a bit foggy to him.

Getting to the microphone, he said boldly, "The greatest years of my life were spent in the arms of a woman that wasn't my wife!"

The congregation was shocked. The pastor stood there in the stunned silence, trying to remember the rest of the joke. He finally blurted out, "...and I can't remember who she was!"

It's better to know all the facts before repeating something – or else you may get yourself into trouble.

April 2

I also saw other things in this life that were not fair. The fastest runner does not always win the race; the strongest soldier does not always win the battle; wise people don't always get the food; smart people don't always get the wealth; educated people don't always get the praise they deserve (Ecclesiastes 9:11, ERV).

Monkey Business

After the British had established colonial power in India, they longed for recreation and decided to build a golf course. But golf in Calcutta presented a unique obstacle...because monkeys would drop out of the trees and pick up the golf balls on the course.

The monkeys would play with the balls for a while, scamper about with them, dropping them all over the course. The British were going nuts. They couldn't stop the monkeys.

Finally, the golfers accepted this unusual disruption of their game. So they added a new rule to the book, which says: "You may play the ball where the monkey drops it."

At times in life, we have to play the ball where the monkey dropped it. It's not always fair. We didn't expect the pathology report, or the pink slip, or the death of a loved one. Press on – no matter where the monkey dropped the ball.

April 3

The fire on the altar shall be kept burning on it; it shall not go out (Leviticus 6:12, ESV).

Trill

Janet was vacationing in the mountains and stopped by the nature center to see the various animals and artifacts that had been discovered in that area.

The final room she visited contained several species of frogs that inhabited the region. She immediately noticed that several of the frogs were making strange sounds, almost like they were singing.

Janet asked one of the naturalist workers about the sound the frogs were making. The naturalist explained, "That is the sound of frogs trilling for a mate. We have a pair in the science room, but they have been together for so long that they no longer sing to each other." The naturalist smiled and added, "The *trill* is gone."

Does it seem like the thrill is gone in your relationship? Do something special for your spouse. Bring in a little excitement, express your love, and do it now. Don't let your relationship lose its *trill*.

April 4

Get wisdom, and whatever you get, get insight (Proverbs 4:7, ESV).

Bucket List Robbery

Many people compile a list of things they want to do before they die. It's called a "bucket list." Typically, people put things on their list like traveling, mending broken relationships, or learning something new.

But Patricia had something a little different on her list. Her bucket list included her wish to rob two banks before she died. So she did. And a few days later, she was arrested.

She said, "It was something on my 'bucket list.' I think everyone should have a list of things they want to do before they die."

Patricia later admitted that she regretted her decision to rob the banks, and she would accept and suffer the consequences. Robbing a bank was on her list. But going to jail was not.

The decisions we make each day will have consequences. Let your bucket list be filled with things that will have a legacy…not larceny.

April 5

Set your minds on things that are above (Colossians 3:2, ESV).

Bird

A young lad caught a bird in his hands. He thought to himself, "I'll go up to the old man over yonder and say, 'Sir, is this bird dead or alive?" If he says, 'He's alive,' I'll squeeze the life out of him. But if the old man says, 'He's dead,' I'll let him fly away." So he went to the old man and said, "Sir, is this bird dead or alive?"

The old man, being wiser than the young boy thought, said, "Son, the future of that bird remains in your hands."

So, it is with our future. We can squeeze the life out of the future through negative thoughts or hopelessness, or we can let ourselves fly away to new dreams, new hopes.

At VOA, that's our mission – to help people find a new hope, a new dream, a new future.

April 6

And if you give even a cup of cold water to one of the least of my followers, you will surely be rewarded (Matthew 10:42, NLT).

Molly Pitcher

Mary was born in 1754 in New Jersey. At 15, she married William Hays, a soldier during the Revolutionary War. When he was called to fight at Valley Forge, Mary did not hesitate to follow him.

During the intense battle, the soldiers soon became hot and thirsty. Wanting to help, Mary carried pitcher after pitcher of cool water to the exhausted soldiers across the hot and bullet-riddled battlefield.

A soldier was injured right before her eyes, and Mary put him onto her back, carrying him to safety. When her husband was wounded, she stepped forward without hesitation and manned his guns...an unprecedented feat for a woman at that time.

When her story reached the ears of George Washington, he was impressed and recognized her as a noncommissioned officer. She became widely known as "Sergeant Molly."

Molly loved her husband and stood by him no matter the circumstances. She did what had to be done and cared about those in need. That's love in deed.

April 7

Everyone who calls on the name of the Lord will be saved
(Romans 10:13, ESV).

Turn Around

Walt was an alcoholic. No one knew the exact cause of his drinking but speculated it stemmed from a hunting accident as a teenager. Walt had accidentally shot his brother, thinking he was a deer. He carried his brother back home and laid him on the porch where he died.

As an adult, Walt stayed drunk… for about six years. It was an embarrassment to his wife and children. One day, Walt went to church and asked God to help him turn his life around and give him 15 years to share the love of God with others.

Walt did just that. He became a pastor, and after preaching for 15 years, he passed away.

He made a difference, I know. He was my grandfather. Just like Walt, we too have the opportunity to change things… change ourselves… with God's help. What would you like to change? Ask God… he is faithful and will answer your call.

April 8

Do not lay up for yourselves treasures on earth, where moth and rust destroy and thieves break in and steal, but lay up . . . treasures in heaven (Matthew 6:19-20, ESV).

Greedy Man

A greedy man sold everything he had to buy a lump of gold. Once he bought it, he decided to bury it in his yard. Every day, he would visit the spot just to look at it.

One of his workmen noticed the man's frequent visits to this particular spot. The workman soon discovered the secret of the hidden treasure, and digging down, came to the lump of gold and stole it.

On his next visit, the greedy man found the hole empty and became hysterical.

A neighbor, seeing him in grief and learning of the cause, told the man to take a stone and place it in the hole. "It will do you quite the same service" the neighbor said, "for when the gold was there, you had it not, as you did not make the slightest use of it."

It is not what you possess; it is what you do with what you have that counts.

April 9

I was afraid, and I went and hid your talent in the ground
(Matthew 25:25, ESV).

Pens

I have a difficult time keeping up with writing pens. Seems like I lose them all the time. I'll pick them up at hotel rooms, and I even lose a hotel pen.

About 20 years ago, a good friend gave me an expensive pen set. I was excited about this wonderful new pen set. But I was afraid that I was going to lose them-- just like I'd lost all the other pens.

So I put the pens neatly away in a safe place. For the past 20 years, they've been safe but not used.

Sometimes our fear of a loss or failure keeps us from using what we have…our talents, resources, or achieving our hopes and dreams. Fear can sometimes paralyze.

But the greatest loss is that for 20 years the purpose of those pens was lost…to safety. Your greatest loss may not be a failure but your failure to use what you have – to be who God created you to be.

April 10

Follow my example, as I follow the example of Christ (1 Corinthians 11:1, NIV).

Billie Burke

Years ago, Billie Burke, the famous actress, was taking a transatlantic ocean trip when she noticed that a man sitting at the table next to her was suffering from a terrible cold.

"Looks like you feel horrible." She said sympathetically. The man nodded. "I'll tell you just what to do for it," she offered.

"Go back to your room and drink lots of orange juice. Take two aspirins. Cover yourself with all the blankets you can find. Sweat the cold out. I know just what I'm talking about. I'm Billie Burke from Hollywood."

The man listened as she spoke, smiled politely and replied, "Thanks. Let me introduce myself; I'm Dr. Mayo from the Mayo clinic."

Who would you listen to? A Hollywood actress or a trained expert? Unfortunately, some Hollywood personalities have more influence in our culture than parents, priests, teachers, or experts. Don't be fooled by the glitz and glamour. Follow the smart ones.

April 11

Blessed is the one who finds wisdom, and the one who gets understanding (Proverbs 3:19, ESV).

Touch of a Button

In a high school physics class, John learned that "AC" meant alternating current. Shortly after graduation, he moved to America and bought his first car. John noticed it had a button marked "AC." He didn't dare touch that button.

Summer was hot, and John drove everywhere with his windows down. One day, he gave a friend a ride, and this friend wondered why the air conditioner was not on.

John explained that the car had no air conditioner. The friend pointed to the "AC" button and told John to push it. John said, "Oh no, that is the alternating current."

But John's friend insisted that he push it. He finally gave in and when he did, his life changed. Relief had been at his fingertips all along!

Are you too afraid to push the right button? Make sure you know what you are doing. Some moves can be cool, and others can be pretty shocking.

April 12

You judge according to the flesh, I judge no one (John 8:15, ESV).

Mr. and Mrs. Stanford

A poorly dressed couple stepped off the train in Boston and walked to the campus of Harvard University. They waited for hours to see the President, who grudgingly agreed to see them.

The lady said, "We had a son who attended Harvard for a year. He loved it here but was accidentally killed. We would like to erect a memorial to him on campus." The President retorted, "Madam, we can't put up statues of everyone who attended Harvard and died!" "Oh, we were thinking about a building," she said. He rolled his eyes. "A building? Have any idea how much a building costs? We have over seven million dollars in the physical plant here at Harvard!"

Turning to her husband, she said, "If that is what it costs to build a university, why don't we start one of our own?" With that, Mr. and Mrs. Leland Stanford went to Palo Alto, California, to establish the university bearing their son's name.

April 13

Greater love has no one than this: to lay down one's life for one's friend (John 15:13, NIV).

Brother Sacrifice

Chad struggled with sickness most of his life. His youngest brother, Ryan, was the opposite: strong, filled with optimism and vitality.

At 27, Chad was diagnosed with an incurable disease that attacks the liver. At 38 years old, he was dying and in need of a liver transplant. His brother Ryan was determined to help.

Ryan's blood typed matched. And the operation would only require a small piece of Ryan's liver to be transplanted…a low-risk procedure.

But something happened. A complication. Ryan did not survive the operation. But Chad is healthy now, with a piece of his brother inside of him. His brother's sacrifice made him whole.

Today Chad struggles with his loss and with his brother's unselfish sacrifice. He wonders, how do I make my life count while honoring him? Am I worth it?

Jesus did the same for us and more. How do we respond?

April 14

Do nothing out of selfish ambition (Philippians 2:3, NIV).

Fairy Wishes

A couple was celebrating their 40th wedding anniversary when a fairy appeared and said, "For loving each other all these years, I will grant you each a wish."

The wife said, "I want to travel around the world with my wonderful husband." Poof! Two plane tickets appeared in her hands.

The husband thought for a moment: "I'm sorry to be selfish, but an opportunity like this may never come again. I wish to have a wife 30 years younger than me."

Poof! The husband became 90 years old.

Selfishness will always make you older than you want to be and take you places you don't want to go.

April 15

You meant evil against me, but God meant it for good
(Genesis 50:20, ESV).

Corrie Ten Boom

Corrie ten Boom was a Dutch woman who helped Jewish refugees during World War II. When her actions were discovered, she and her family were imprisoned in Nazi concentration camps.

She endured tremendous sufferings and horrors in these camps. Many of her fellow prisoners, her friends, including her sister and father, were executed.

At one camp, in particular, the conditions were horrible. The tent was overcrowded. The tent was also infested with fleas. Every day the prisoners endured the fleas with no relief.

Corrie couldn't understand why the fleas. Wasn't the torture enough? But because the fleas were so bad, the guards stopped coming into the tents. These prisoners did not have to endure the abuse from the guards. What was an irritation was really protection.

What Corrie ten Boom could not understand at the moment, later she understood. Be patient. God is always working – trust in Him, you will see His hand at work.

April 16

This is love: not that we loved God, but that he loved us and sent his Son as an atoning sacrifice for our sins (1 John 4:10, NIV).

Welfare to Work

Martha Hawkins can tell you how important it is to believe in yourself. A young mother of three, living in public housing, on welfare, and without hope for a better life, attempted suicide. While confined to a psychiatric hospital, she found a Bible and found herself. Her testimony is --when she learned that God loved her, she learned to love herself. Then she found hope and a dream.

Today her restaurant is the toast of Montgomery. Governors, members of Congress, key leaders from around the state and nation enjoy her cooking. Her story has been told in major newspapers and magazines. Also, she has appeared on Oprah. She serves as an inspirational model to all who aspire to a better standard of living.

It all started when the young welfare mother started believing in herself and her God. With simple faith and hard work, she moved from welfare to business ownership.

April 17

He is not here, for he has risen (Matthew 28:6, ESV).

Jesus Resurrection

Easter is a time to celebrate the resurrection of Jesus Christ! The significance of Easter is that Jesus died for our sins, experienced darkness for us, and was resurrected. Now He is alive and well and has sent the Holy Spirit as our comforter.

You may be feeling weary, depressed, or going through tough times, but remember, Jesus can resurrect us spiritually, emotionally, and even physically, as we carry a relationship with Him!

As we celebrate Easter every Sunday, let us remember that we don't have to carry our burdens. Jesus says, "Come to me, all you who are weary and burdened, and I will give you rest. For my yoke is easy, and my burden is light."

Jesus already paid the price. Surrender to Him and experience the true joy and the resurrection He has for you.

April 18

In the last days there will come times of difficulty (2 Timothy 3:1, ESV).

Tinkerbell

It was a very windy Saturday in Michigan. Dorothy and her husband were at the flea market setting up an outdoor display. They had brought their six-pound chihuahua with them, Tinkerbell.

Tinkerbell was happily standing by, watching her owners set up their display, when suddenly, a strong gust of wind lifted her and carried her out of sight.

Tinkerbell was later found about a mile away in a wooded area. Her brown fur was matted and dirty. She was hungry but otherwise okay. When reunited with her family, she began jumping for joy.

The winds of change can sometimes take us by surprise. Challenges and difficulties can blow us off course and often carry us further away than we want to go.

But don't despair; reach out for help from your friends, your family. Someone is there to help you brush off the dirt and keep going.

April 19

Delight yourself in the LORD, and he will give you the desires of your heart (Psalm 37:4, ESV).

Delight

We are all incomplete, with a hole that can only be filled by God. Our souls are eternal, and that's why the things of this world can never fully satisfy.

It's often greed and selfishness that drive us to seek fulfillment in other things. Greed is at the root of our current economic state, Wall Street, foreclosures, overwhelming debt, drug addictions, alcoholism, destroyed marriages. And these things only leave us less satisfied.

We must remember that our souls were meant only to be filled by God. We can never overdose on Him. A relationship with God won't require medical attention; rather, it can add years to your life.

He will never foreclose on us when we fail him. We will never have to tear down our barns and build greater storage for His delights. When we delight in Him, He will never cease to be enough.

April 20

I will forgive their iniquity, and I will remember their sin no more (Jeremiah 31:34, ESV).

Bury the Past

Have you heard the phrase "bury the hatchet?" This expression originated as a Native American tradition. When tribe chiefs came to a peace agreement, they buried their hatchets in the ground.

The practice is recorded in historical documents. Native American tribes buried their hatchets in a ceremony that was considered very significant and binding. It became an unbreakable covenant of peace between two rival tribes.

Many of us need to bury the hatchet…but not in the person who did you wrong. Maybe it was a nasty divorce that took place. Maybe it's a family member or friend that never repaid money they borrowed. Maybe it was unkind words said about you.

Whatever hurt and pain that was caused in the past, forgiveness, and peace will change your life. Whatever it is, bury the hatchet today. Bury the hatchet where you will never find it, and it does no one harm.

April 21

Let each of you look not only to his own interests, but also to the interests of others (Philippians 2:4, ESV).

Terminal Husband

An elderly couple went to the doctor, concerned about the husband's health. After the examination, the doctor met with the wife alone.

"It is serious," he told her. "So much depends on you and how motivated you are. You must pamper him, prepare special foods for him, allow him to express his anger, let him nap, and above all, allow him to have his own way, so he doesn't become agitated."

She left the doctor's office very concerned. When she and her husband were driving home, he asked his wife what the doctor had said.

She looked at him and replied, "I hate to tell you this, but based on what the doctor said, it looks like you are probably not going to make it."

None of us will make it without love and kindness, even in the best of times. What kind of person would you be if you lived like today is your last day?

April 22

He guides me along the right paths for his name's sake
(Psalm 23:3, NIV).

Guidance

I pray every day for God's guidance. In the word guidance is the word *dance*. The first three letters—*gui*—could mean "God, you and I dance."

In a dance, the leader gently nudges their partner across the dance floor in a beautiful dance. The partner must follow the other's lead. If both try to lead...the whole dance is thrown off.

Pray for God's guidance today. Let Him lead you. Psalm 23 says: The Lord is my shepherd; I shall not want. He makes me lie down in green pastures, he leads me beside quiet waters, He restores my soul. He guides me in paths of righteousness for his name's sake. Even though I walk through the valley of the shadow of death, I will fear no evil, for you are with me; your rod and your staff, they comfort me.

Let God lead your dance today.

April 23

Suffering produces perseverance (Romans 5:3, NIV).

Bear Grylls

Edward had always been an avid outdoorsman. Growing up in Britain, his lifelong dream was to climb Mount Everest.

When he graduated college, he joined the British Special Forces. But one day, while freefalling, his parachute pack did not open. He landed on his back, breaking it in three places.

Would he ever walk again? Doubtful. What about his dream to climb Mt Everest? Not likely.

But he didn't quit; he didn't give up. Eighteen months later, at the age of 23, he climbed Mount Everest. Today he holds the Guinness World Record for the youngest Briton to climb Mount Everest.

Since then, he has led record-breaking expeditions across the world. You have probably heard of him. He's Bear Grylls of the show *Man vs. Wild.*

When life knocks you on your back, don't give up. Set goals and work to achieve them. Be an inspiration to those around you.

April 24

Do to others what you would have them do to you
(Matthew 7:12, NIV).

Competitors

Eric and Barbara Havill returned to upstate New York in 1972. They bought a dilapidated farmhouse and spent the next several years making it livable. They opened a pottery studio and spent many years building a pottery business, and they became known for their quality work.

Years later, Ray and Monica Sommerville opened Sommerville Pottery Studio in this same small community.

In a recent visit to Eric's studio's I was amazed when he said, as we were leaving, "You need to go over to Sommerville Pottery Studio. They do nice work."

What if all competitors were like Eric? You don't always see that graciousness to a newcomer. We now are a county that longs for such kindness.

We talk about the political divisiveness in our country and how we need to work together. But as we are complaining, we need to remember that we must be kind even to those who sell the same product as we do.

April 25

Better to live in a desert than with a quarrelsome and nagging wife [or husband] (Proverbs 21:19, NIV).

Nagging

A woman and her nagging husband went on vacation to Jerusalem to visit the Holy Land. While they were there, the husband passed away.

The undertaker told the woman, "You can have him shipped home for $5,000, or you can bury him here, in the Holy Land, for $150." The wife thought about it for a moment and told the undertaker that she would just pay the $5,000 and have him shipped home.

Surprised by her answer, the undertaker asked, "Why would you spend $5,000 to ship your husband home? It would be wonderful to bury him here in the Holy Land, and you would spend only $150!" The woman replied, "Long ago, a man died here, was buried here, and three days later, he rose from the dead. I just can't take that chance."

Stop the nagging. Take a chance with your husband or your wife…live before you die. You'll like it.

April 26

I am setting before you today a blessing (Deuteronomy 11:26, ESV).

Bad day

We all have bad days. I read recently that you really know it's going to be a bad day when:

- You wake up face down on the pavement.
- You see a 60 Minutes news team waiting in your office.
- You turn on the news, and they're showing emergency routes out of the city.
- Your twin sister forgets your birthday.
- You wake up to discover that your waterbed broke and then realized you don't have a waterbed.
- Your horn goes off accidentally and remains stuck as you follow a group of Hell's Angels on the freeway.

The next time you have a bad day, remember that you are probably more blessed than you realize. Don't focus too much on the things that go wrong. Instead, focus on your blessings. You will find that sometimes your bad day may not be as bad as you thought.

April 27

In due season we will reap if we do not give up (Galatians 6:9, ESV).

Adam Emily

For the seven years that I have known Adam, age 25, he has been on the hunt—for a wife. When he found her, he wanted to propose marriage as soon as possible.

Adam bought her a ring. Emily would be totally surprised.

He had it all planned!!!!! It was going to be the most romantic evening ever!!! He had a canopy, a glass table with two chairs, and white lights were everywhere. He had a candlelight dinner planned for the evening!!! It was the perfect night to have it outside. He brought in seafood from her favorite restaurant. Everything was going great!!! It was perfect!

The only problem, Emily didn't show! Poor Adam.

The rest of the story. A week later she accepted, and they were later married. Don't give up on your dreams when they first appear to be a no-show.

April 28

The fear of the LORD is the beginning of wisdom (Psalm 111:10, ESV).

Cowboy Wisdom

Have you heard any wisdom lately? Here is some cowboy wisdom I recently read:

- Life is not about how fast you run or how high you climb, but how well you bounce.
- Life is simpler when you plow around the stump.
- Words that soak in your ears are whispered, not yelled.
- Meanness don't happen overnight.
- Every path has some puddles.
- The best sermons are lived, not preached.
- Most of the stuff people worry about never happens.
- Live a good, honorable life. Then when you get older and think back, you'll enjoy it a second time.
- Good judgment comes from experience and a lotta that comes from bad judgment.
- Lettin' the cat outta the bag is a whole lot easier than puttin' it back in.

Some good wisdom comes from life's experiences. But the Psalmist said, "The fear of the Lord is the beginning of wisdom."

April 29

Doesn't… discrimination show that your judgments are guided by evil motives? (James 2:4, NLT).

Pop Quiz

During nursing school, a professor gave his students a pop quiz. The class was very attentive during lectures and breezed through most of the quiz with ease.

However, the last question stumped them. It read, "What is the first name of the woman who cleans the school?" Surely this is a joke, they thought. They had seen the cleaning woman several times. She was tall, dark-haired and in her 50's, but her name? They didn't know.

Just before class ended, one student asked if the last question would count toward their quiz grade. "Absolutely," said the professor. "In your careers, you will meet many people. All are significant. They deserve your attention and care, even if all you do is smile and say 'hello.'

That was perhaps one of the most significant lessons the class learned that year. They also learned that her name was Dorothy. Today would be a great day to learn someone's name.

April 30

Be doers of the word and not hearers only (James 1:22, ESV).

Sad Story

Once there was a young boy who said to his family, "I want to do great things with my life, and I know I can."

Many years later, an old man said to his family, "I could have done great things with my life. I wish I had."

This is a sad story because the young boy and the old man were the same person.

Don't let this be your story! As motivational speaker Rob Gilbert says, "It's never too late – to do something great!"

It may sound trite, but today is the first day of the rest of your life. You can make choices today that have greatness in them. You can choose to make a difference in another person's life. You can bless others by your words and your deeds. There is always greatness present when someone reaches out to help another.

May 1

Therefore they shall eat the fruit of their way, and have their fill of their own devices (Proverbs 1:31, ESV).

Entitlements

We live in the age of entitlement. We're entitled to this and entitled to that—and somebody else should pay for it.

We see this throughout all walks of life and all ages. The children of the rich say, "Buy me a car and a house too." The poor mother says, "Pay for my babies." We live in an entitlement culture.

Entitlement is what has driven this country into deep debt. Big businesses want exemptions and bailouts. The media tells consumers to purchase this and buy that…because we deserve it. But entitlements are destroying our economy and personal budgets.

You might say, "this isn't me." But you may be wrong. Our culture has an ingrained attitude of entitlement and rights. So much so that we don't even notice, it's become a way of life. The new American Way.

Our Constitution entitles us to "Life, liberty and the pursuit of happiness." What more could you want?

May 2

Examine yourselves, to see whether you are in the faith (2 Corinthians 13:5, ESV).

1000 Mirrors

Long ago, in a tiny village, there was a place known as the House of 1000 Mirrors. One day, a happy little dog decided to visit. When he arrived, he found himself staring at 1000 other happy little dogs with their tails wagging just as fast as his.

He smiled a great big smile and, in turn, saw 1000 smiles just as warm. As he left the house, he thought, "This is a wonderful place. I will come back and visit again."

Another dog, who was quite grumpy, decided to visit the house. When he looked in, he saw 1000 unfriendly-looking dogs staring back at him. He growled at the dogs and, in turn, saw 1000 dogs growling back at him.

As he left, he thought, "That is a horrible place, and I'll never go back there again."

What kind of reflections will you see in the faces of the people you meet?

May 3

Therefore encourage one another and build one another up, just as you are doing (1 Thessalonians 5:11, ESV).

Coach Cheeks

In 2003, at the Portland Trailblazers/Dallas Mavericks basketball game, 13-year-old Natalie was asked to sing the national anthem in front of 20,000 fans. But as she stepped up to the microphone to sing, she forgot the words. That's when the Portland Trailblazers Coach, Maurice Cheeks, walked over to Natalie, put his arm around her, and began to sing the words with her.

Soon, the 20,000 fans in the arena joined in. At the end of the anthem, Coach Cheeks gave Natalie a hug and told her not to worry – that everyone has a bad game every now and then.

Coach Cheeks saw Natalie's need for support, and he didn't hesitate to step in and encourage her to keep going despite her mistake. What could have been an embarrassment for Natalie turned into a moment of triumph.

When someone needs encouragement, don't hesitate to step in and help. Turning tragedy into triumph…that sounds like music to my ears.

May 4

God is unto us a God of deliverances (Psalm 68:20, ASV).

Audrey Hepburn

It was 1935, and little Audrey was six years old. She and her mother moved to the Netherlands to help the Dutch Resistance during the Nazi regime.

Times were very difficult for Audrey and her mom. Her father was a Nazi sympathizer and had left them. They were often close to starvation, sometimes eating tulip bulbs out of desperation. Audrey's cousin and uncle were both executed, and her brother was sent to a Nazi concentration camp. Several of her friends were imprisoned.

Audrey's job was to carry food and coded messages to Allied soldiers. On one occasion, she was on her way to deliver information to an Allied pilot when she encountered a Nazi soldier. But she was able to convince him that she was simply in the woods to pick daisies.

That's how little Audrey Hepburn learned to give great performances.

It is often in difficult circumstances that our greatest potential can be discovered.

May 5

Until now you have asked nothing in my name. Ask, and you will receive, that your joy may be full (John 16:24, ESV).

The Pain of a Parent

Years ago, I made a home visit to see the daughter of an older couple. Ollie and Lucy had been parents to Connie for 42 years. Connie had cerebral palsy, weighed 50 lbs, and required total care. Her mother had been hospitalized, and Ollie could not take care of both. He needed help.

What amazed me was that for 42 years, this couple had cared for their daughter without hesitation, doing everything they could under long and trying circumstances. Connie went to a great care facility. She outlived her parents and recently died, but not without a life of love and care by her family.

How we deal with difficulties makes all the difference in who we are and who we become.

Sometimes when our loads are heavy, the only thing we can do is stay under the load. Sometimes we have to call for help.

May 6

Wisdom is with the aged, and understanding in length of days (Job 12:12, ESV).

Life 101

Marvin Northen left Baylor University in 1929, one credit shy of graduating with a degree in chemistry.

He left Baylor because the Great Depression had hit, and he needed to work to help his family. He never went back to finish. But as Marvin Northen celebrated his 100th birthday, he was finally granted his degree.

He had a surprise graduation ceremony at his church when he was presented with a diploma, a cap and gown, and his official transcript.

According to the university, Northen had been participating in a class that could be substituted for the Chemistry class that he never took. The class? Life 101. He mastered that course well and passed with a grade of A-plus, without even knowing it.

Perhaps the university recognized something that we often fail to do…that's honoring our elders. We could learn a lot from those around us who have a wisdom that can only be found in a long and full life.

May 7

Truly I tell you, if you have faith as small as a mustard seed, you can say to this mountain, "Move from here to there," and it will move (Matthew 17:20, NIV).

The Unbreakable Barrier

By 1954, numerous medical journals had published articles saying that running the mile in less than four minutes was not humanly possible. Doctors warned of the dangers for anyone who broke that "unbreakable barrier." Even coaches told their athletes to forget about breaking the "impossible" barrier.

However, in May 1954, Roger Bannister ran a mile in less than four minutes, which ignited the athletic world. In 1994, Emon Coglan of Ireland did it again.

Roger Bannister broke the barrier and changed that thinking by his performance. He did not listen to what others said. He didn't want to limit his potential. He believed in himself. He proved that the barrier was psychological, not physiological. Dr. Jerry Lynch said that when you believe and think "I can," you activate your motivation, commitment, and confidence, all of which are directly related to achievement.

Believe in yourself, and you can move mountains.

May 8

They still bear fruit in old age; they are ever full of sap and green (Psalm 92:14, ESV).

George Blanda

George Blanda began his football career at the University of Kentucky under Bear Bryant. He signed on to play for the Chicago Bears, but an injury took him off as starting quarterback and place-kicker. Many said that Blanda, at best, had five more years of a pro-football career.

But he proved them wrong. Blanda left the NFL and joined the AFL with the Houston Oilers as quarterback and kicker. The media called him an "NFL reject."

Blanda went on to lead the Oilers to the first two league titles in AFL history, and he even won the AFL Player of the Year. Blanda led his team to many more victories, earning him the AFL's Most Valuable Player award.

He retired at the age of 49 as the oldest quarterback in pro football. More recently, Tom Brady led the Tampa Bay Buccaneers to a Super Bowl LV victory at age 43.

You're never too old to be your best.

May 9

Truly, truly, I say to you, when you were young, you used to dress yourself and walk wherever you wanted, but when you are old, you will stretch out your hands, and another will dress you and carry you (John 21:18, ESV).

Mrs. Johnson

She had raised her family well. The boys were all grown and gone. Now, it was just her and her husband. Time to retire and kick back.

Mrs. Johnson decided to have that old hip replaced. Just a typical hip replacement. It went well. And then on the second day, she had a stroke. It changed their lives. She had been the caregiver—each son thought he was the favorite, and each son knew that his mom was the best cook. But the roles changed. Suddenly, the mother who had given so much to her family had to learn to receive, and those who had received so much had to learn to give more than ever.

As her son said, "She taught us through her example what we would do for her." So, Mrs. Johnson, let them give to you the same way that you taught. Children, remember to honor your mothers and demonstrate that there are no limits to caring for your family.

May 10

Be faithful unto death, and I will give you the crown of life (Revelation 2:10, ESV).

Faithful

With the passing of my daddy, there is a lesson that I learned along the way…"faithful to the end." In the last years, Daddy's focus was on taking care of Mama. She had Alzheimer's. More than anything, his goal was to take care of Mama at home until the end. And, no doubt, that was his biggest challenge of his life.

After years of caring for Mama, his own dementia, Lewy Body Disease, took over and we had to provide a different kind of care…it was difficult for each of us. But we came to the edge and we made the tough decisions…And they received good care…and he still did what he could for her.

In the health care facility, you could see him pushing Mama to the dining room or back to their room…always telling the nurses what Mama really needed…her advocate to the end.

Till death do us part…66 years later, and that commitment still was there.

May 11

A man who has friends must himself be friendly (Proverbs 18:24, NKJ).

Neighbors

Johnny didn't know his neighbors, but he was friendly and would wave or say hello in passing. One day, a social media site linked him to people with the same interests. He was excited to meet people that enjoyed the same hobbies.

Through social media, Johnny became good friends with Bill. They both liked baseball and football and would talk about their favorite teams.

One day, a thunderstorm caused Johnny's power to go out. When the power came back on, he discovered that Bill's electricity went out too! After sharing their addresses, the two men learned that they lived on the same street!

How well do we know our neighbors? Not too many years ago, before air conditioners, computers, and cell phones…we opened our windows, went outside, and talked with the neighbors. Jesus was asked the question, "Who is my neighbor?"

Who are your neighbors? You might like them if you get to know them.

May 12

Keep all the promises you make (Ecclesiastes 5:4, NLT).

A Promise

Staff Sgt Roberto Loeza, Jr. was an Infantry Rifle Squad Leader. He was deployed to Afghanistan in 2011. Before he left, he made a promise to his youngest sister, Lluvia, that he would be at her high school graduation. But unfortunately, he could not keep that promise. He died from injuries in battle.

Roberto's brother Esteban wanted to surprise his sister at her graduation. He sent a message to Roberto's old unit, many back in Afghanistan, and asked them to stand in Roberto's place. More than 30 soldiers attended the graduation.

His sister was completely surprised to see the soldiers gathered in Army Uniforms. The Battalion Executive officer was given permission to present Lluvia with her high school diploma. And then all the soldiers stood and saluted her.

A brother kept a promise in a unique way.

May 13

Lift up your hands to the holy place, and bless the Lord!
(Psalm 134:2, RSV).

Whose Hands

A basketball in my hands is worth about $19.
A basketball in Michael Jordan's hands is worth about $33 million.
It depends on whose hands it's in.

A baseball in my hands is worth about $6.
A baseball in Mark McGuire's hands is worth $19 million.
It depends on whose hands it's in.

A tennis racket is useless in my hands.
A tennis racket in Serena Williams' hands is a Championship.
It depends on whose hands it's in.

Two fish and five loaves of bread in my hands are a couple of fish sandwiches.
Two fish and five loaves of bread in the hands of Jesus Christ fed thousands.
It depends on whose hands it's in.

What are you doing with what's in your hands? Today is a great day to build up, to bless, to create, and to help. It's all about what's in your hands and what you're doing with it.

May 14

All day long he craves and craves, but the righteous gives and does not hold back (Proverbs 21:26, ESV).

Woman in Attic

Bob was a busy man. He worked long hours, many times leaving for work while it was still dark and arriving home late at night.

He began to notice that some of his food was missing, and things were sometimes out of place. So he installed cameras and transmitted the images to his office. To his surprise, he saw a burglar in his home, eating food out of his pantry. So he phoned the police and rushed home.

But when they arrived, the doors and windows were locked. They searched the entire house for the intruder and found a woman in the attic.

She explained that she was homeless, with nowhere to go, and had been living in Bob's attic for over a year – as if it were her own home.

Sometimes we become so busy that:
- we don't know what is happening in our own pantry
- or we fail to see those who are hungry.

May 15

I would be acquitted forever by my judge (Job 23:7, ESV).

Death Penalty

What can one teacher do? Perhaps more than we know. Since 1992, David Protess has challenged his journalism students to investigate the circumstances of convicted criminals. His undergraduate students have helped to free seven innocent men.

One was Anthony Porter, who had just two days to live. The state of Illinois stayed his execution, and a few months later, the real killer confessed. Porter walked out of prison a free man.

This journalism teacher and his students were a driving force behind Republican Illinois governor George Ryan's decision to suspend executions until Ryan says he "can be sure that everyone sentenced to death in Illinois is truly guilty."

What can one person do to make a difference? It starts by caring enough about an issue or a cause to actually get involved. Just one teacher, caring enough, making a powerful difference here and now and around the country.

May 16

The LORD is my strength and my shield; in him my heart trusts and I am helped (Psalm 28:7, ESV).

Sean Swarner

When Sean Swarner was 13, he was diagnosed with Hodgkin's disease and given three months to live.

When he was 15, he was diagnosed with Askin's Sarcoma. This time, the doctors gave him only two weeks to live. Again, he survived.

On May 16, 2002, Sean became the first (and only) cancer survivor to summit the world's highest mountain... Mount Everest.

Since then, he has reached the summits of three more of the world's highest peaks. His ultimate goal is to climb the highest mountain on each continent and go to the North and South poles.

Being the only person in the world to have ever had these two cancers, he has shared his story to help motivate others and influence lives.

Why does he do it? Sean has a passion to inspire those affected by cancer to dream big and never give up. Live by that motto...dream big and never give up...no matter the adversities.

May 17

Keep your life free from love of money, and be content with what you have, for he has said, "I will never leave you nor forsake you" (Hebrews 13:5, ESV).

Enough

Janet was waiting for her flight at the airport when she saw a mother and daughter saying goodbye. Standing near the security gate, they hugged, and the mother said, "I love you, and I pray you enough."

They kissed, and the daughter left. The mother walked over to the window near Janet and began to talk to Janet.

The mother explained that she had health problems and her daughter lived far away, busy with her family and career. Her daughter's next trip back would probably be for the mother's funeral.

Janet asked why the mom told her daughter that she prayed her enough. The mother told her that the prayer was for the other person to have a life filled with just enough good things to sustain them.

In our culture, we are never satisfied with what we have. When we surround ourselves with loved ones, all we need is just enough good things to sustain us.

May 18

For what thanksgiving can we return to God for you, for all the joy that we feel for your sake before our God (1 Thessalonians 3:9, ESV).

Supporting Cast

The motion picture industry gives Academy Awards each year for those who excel in that business. International attention is given to these awards, and everyone wants to know the winner for Best Movie, Best Actor, and Best Actress.

Awards are also given to an actor and actress for Best Supporting Role. Rabbi Harold Kushner, in a recent book, invites us to think about the "Supporting Actors" in OUR lives. We all have them. People whose lives have touched us in ways that make our lives better. Spouses, parents, teachers, friends, and sometimes even strangers, who have offered encouragement, and provided opportunities for us.

Kushner suggests we should issue our own "Best Supporting" awards to those who have enabled us to have better lives. Good idea. It doesn't have to be a statue or certificate. A simple thank you might just prove to be award enough.

May 19

Do not forget to show hospitality to strangers, for by so doing some people have shown hospitality to angels without knowing it (Hebrews 13:2, NIV).

Guardian Angel

Yvonne was flying home and had a short layover in Atlanta. As she was waiting for her connecting flight, she came upon an elderly lady who was obviously lost or confused.

Yvonne asked her what flight she was taking. When the lady showed Yvonne her ticket, Yvonne realized she was on the wrong concourse.

Yvonne explained that she needed to take the train to another concourse to catch her flight. The elderly lady asked, "Train? What train?"

So, Yvonne walked the elderly lady to the elevator, rode with her on the train, and guided her directly to her flight…with only moments to spare. As the elderly lady boarded her flight, she stopped, turned back to Yvonne, hugged her and said, "You are my guardian angel."

There are <u>many more</u> opportunities for <u>you</u> to be a guardian angel. Look around you…there are divine opportunities for you today… be a guardian angel. There are no limits to caring.

May 20

Trust in the Lord with all your heart, and do not lean on your own understanding. In all your ways acknowledge him, and he will make straight your paths (Proverbs 3:5-6, ESV).

Reagan

When Ronald Reagan was a young boy, his aunt took him to shop for a pair of new shoes. The shoemaker asked young Reagan, "Do you want square toes or round toes?" Reagan was unable to decide, so the shoemaker gave him a few days to decide.

Several days later, the shoemaker asked Reagan again what kind of toes he wanted on his shoes. Reagan still couldn't decide.

So the shoemaker replied, "Come by the store in a few days. Your shoes will be ready." When the future president went to pick up his shoes, he found one square-toed shoe and one round-toed shoe!

The shoemaker told young Reagan, "This will teach you to never let people make decisions for you." Reagan later said, "I learned right then and there if you don't make your own decisions, someone else will."

When we let others make our decisions, the result may not be what we like. Know what you want. Consult the best. Make wise, decisive decisions.

May 21

There are doubtless many different languages in the world, and none is without meaning (1 Corinthians 14:10, ESV).

No Problem

When you were young, before you left kindergarten, you learned to say "thank you" and "you are welcome." A few years ago, my new young assistant would always reply with "no problem" instead of "you are welcome."

This was different; I didn't understand what that meant. It seemed a little out of place. Was it rude? Impolite? That was a different way for me to hear "you're welcome." But the phrase "you are welcome" actually means, "You are under no obligation for the favor given."

From the younger generation to the older generation, there is a difference in how we express ourselves both in words and in actions. Perhaps in place of trying to change either generation, we should embrace those differences.

Our differences tend to be our battlegrounds. Instead, we must embrace and celebrate those differences.

Celebrate your differences; don't spend time trying to change those around you. Embrace and celebrate your differences.

May 22

Gracious words are like a honeycomb, sweetness to the soul and health to the body (Proverbs 16:24, ESV).

Barking Dogs

I ride my bike or walk as a way of exercise. I always meet up with a number of dogs…some friendly and some not. Some always bark at me, and some just wag their tails and run along beside me.

The other day after having had a number of dogs bark at me, I came home to my neighbor's barking dog. And the owner said, "He's has already been barked at today…no need for you to bark."

What if we had that attitude when our children got home from school… "They have already been barked at…no need for me to bark." Or what if when your spouse came home… "no need to bark…she's already been barked at."

We live in a dog-eat-dog world…and most likely, someone has been barking at our children…our spouse.

What we each need is not a bark, but a hug, a word of affirmation, a word of appreciation, encouragement.

May 23

If God so clothes the grass of the field, which today is alive and tomorrow is thrown into the oven, will he not much more clothe you (Matthew 6:30, ESV).

Big Foot God

ZR was wounded in Iraq. He is from Lineville, Alabama. He had to return home for surgery. He flew from Kuwait to Germany with his bags. When he left Germany headed home, he went through customs. His tennis shoes were on top in one of his bags. When he got to Atlanta and went through customs, his tennis shoes were gone.

After he arrived at the hospital, the chaplain asked him if he needed anything. ZR told him his tennis shoes were stolen. The chaplain asked him what size, and ZR told him. The chaplain said, "I have a pair of those." Not really a big deal until you know that his shoes are a size 15. Now that's a big foot!

Could your faith say that God, through his people, can take care of small details like big shoes—when God has such a big mess going on everywhere else?

May 24

Be good husbands to your wives. Honor them, delight in them (1 Peter 3:7, MSG).

Knowing Your Mate

While attending a marriage seminar on communication, David and his wife listened to the instructor declare, "It is essential that husbands and wives know the things that are important to each other."

He addressed the man, "Can you describe your wife's favorite flower?" David leaned over, touched his wife's arm, and gently and whispered, "Pillsbury All-Purpose, isn't it?"

What's your husband's favorite food? What's your wife's greatest fear?

Knowing one another is the beginning of a great relationship. Without that knowledge, nothing really good can happen.

His Needs, Her Needs by William F. Harley is a great book that helps couples to understand each other's needs. Try this book, learn the favorite need of your mate—then go for it! You'll be glad you did—and so will your family!!

May 25

You shall stand up before the gray head and honor the face of an old man, and you shall fear your God: I am the Lord (Leviticus 19:32, ESV).

Eileen Nearne

Most of us have never heard of Eileen Nearne. She died a few years ago in Britain, an elderly woman, poor and alone.

After her death, officials discovered several medals of honor in her home. It turns out that during World War 2, she had been a female agent for the Royal British Legion. She had been a war heroine, risking her life, working undercover.

Recruited for her language skills, she worked undercover in France. She was captured several times by the Germans, sent to concentration camps, and narrowly escaped.

After the war, she lived alone and never discussed her past with any of her neighbors…never made friends or had a family.

Many older people have amazing secrets and abundant wisdom to share. But many are lonely and isolated…no family and no connections. Be a family to an older person.

Do not forget them. Be a blessing and be blessed.

May 26

A man of many companions may come to ruin, but there is a friend who sticks closer than a brother (Proverbs 18:24, ESV).

Crisis

What do you do when you have a crisis in your life? Where do you turn?

Do you remember this nursery rhyme? Humpty Dumpty sat on a wall. Humpty Dumpty had a great fall. All the King's horses and all the King's men couldn't put Humpty together again.

What was Humpty's crisis? He fell off a wall. No government official could put him back together. None of the King's horses nor any of the Kings' men could put Humpty together again.

We each have a fear of falling…..we dream about falling. We will fall. But what then? Sometimes life is more about how we get up than how many times we fall. A crisis doesn't have to be the end.

When it falls apart with your marriage…what then? When the kids experiment with drugs? Your job is falling apart?

Find a spiritual friend, turn to your faith in God. He's in the business of putting back together what you cannot fix.

May 27

Many are the afflictions of the righteous, but the LORD delivers him out of them all (Psalm 34:19, ESV).

Superman

Christopher Reeve, best known for his role as Superman, became a paraplegic following an accident at age 42. He died at the age of 52.

Ironically, he played a paraplegic in a film seven months before his accident. To prepare for the role, he worked with patients in a rehab center. He would leave thinking, "Thank God, that's not me." Then a few months later, it WAS him.

He said, "We are all one great big family, and any one of us can get hurt at any moment. We should never walk by somebody who's in a wheelchair and be afraid of them, or think of them as a stranger." Reeve said, "It could be us—in fact, it is us."

Christopher Reeve learned valuable lessons the hard way and taught us lessons as well. (1) It can be me at any time. (2) Ever how difficult the path, fight a good fight. Never give up.

May 28

This is my commandment, that you love one another as I have loved you (John 15:12, ESV).

Can I Help?

Dr. Doug Lawson tells of having car trouble while traveling through France. Not knowing what to do, he asked a Dutch couple in a travel trailer nearby for help. Although they spoke no English, they tried but could not start the car.

A German-speaking couple offered to assist, but they too were unsuccessful. Forty-five minutes later, a Belgian truck driver and several others who spoke no English stopped. At last, the car started. The gathered crowd cheered, and everyone went on their way.

Through that experience, Dr. Lawson said that he just might have discovered how to achieve world peace. He said, "Give us all something for which to volunteer, and all the artificial boundaries of hate and fear and distrust will dissolve into that exciting moment when one human being says to another, 'Can I help?'"

If you want to spread a little world peace today, offer a helping hand to someone.

May 29

Wait for the Lord; be strong, and let your heart take courage; wait for the Lord! (Psalm 27:14, ESV).

Crossroads

One day during World War I, Winston Churchill visited France to see the front lines. In his shelter on the front line, he received a message that a visiting general wanted to see him.

Churchill was instructed to meet the general at a crossroads three miles away. He waited at the crossroads for nearly an hour when one of the general's officers pulled up.

The officer explained that the general had accidentally gone to the wrong crossroads, and it was now too late for any meeting to take place. Aggravated, Churchill returned to his camp on the front lines. He was shocked to find that his shelter had been bombed a few minutes before.

Sometimes in life, the things that aggravate us the most can actually be a blessing. If life has you at a crossroads and your options leave you waiting, don't be aggravated or impatient. Wait on God and see the blessings he has for you.

May 30

Remember the wondrous works that he has done, his miracles and the judgments he uttered (1 Chronicles 16:12, ESV).

Don't Forget to Remember

Two middle-aged couples were enjoying friendly conversation when one of the men asked the other, "Fred, how was the memory clinic you went to last month?"

"Outstanding," Fred replied. "They taught us all the latest psychological techniques, such as visualization, association, and so on. It was great. I haven't had a problem since."

"Sounds like something I could use. What was the name of the clinic?"

Fred went blank. He thought and thought but couldn't remember. Then a smile broke across his face and he asked, "What do you call that flower with the long stem and thorns?"

"You mean a rose?" "Yes, that's it!" He turned to his wife, "Hey Rose, what was the name of that memory clinic?"

Sometimes we fail to remember the really important things in life like… our blessings…the kindness of others, or even those that remember the important things in life…like there are no limits to caring.

May 31

For he himself is our peace, who has made the two groups one and has destroyed the barrier, the dividing wall of hostility (Ephesians 2:14, NIV).

Confederation Bridge

Prince Edward Island, off the coast of Canada, could only be reached by boat. It was too dangerous to build a bridge to the island because of the strong currents and icy waters.

It seemed impossible to build a bridge that would stand such conditions. Many gave up on building a bridge. It seemed impossible!

But the dream of linking the island to the mainland was one that would not be given up lightly. After years of planning and hard work, a bridge was constructed, taking four years to complete. The bridge is 14 miles long and is the longest bridge over ice-covered waters in the world.

Perhaps in our own personal lives, we need to build bridges…to people. The previous relationship may be icy, cold, intimidating, and impossible. But with determination, you can build a bridge, even over strong currents of resentment and anger.

Build a bridge and explore what's on the other side.

June 1

Let him kiss me with the kisses of his mouth—for your love is more delightful than wine (Song of Solomon 1:2, NIV).

A Record Marriage

A British couple set a Guinness World Record in 2005. Eighty years of marriage. Percy, age 105, and Florence, age 100, were married June 1st, 1925. They made vows of love and commitment 80 years ago! They say there are two secrets to making a marriage last: first, never go to bed mad, and second remember the words, "I'm sorry."

Florence said, "We kiss every night. He can't settle if I'm not holding his hand." Imagine having that much love after 80 years. We could learn a lot from Percy and Florence. Always remember the vows you made to your spouse and honor them.

Marriage is not always easy; it takes work and respect. Sometimes it's not who was wrong but who is willing to say, "I'm sorry." Those two little words can mean so much. Remember to tell your spouse how much you love them – it will make a marriage.

June 2

Let all who take refuge in you be glad; let them ever sing for joy. Spread your protection over them (Psalms 5;11, NIV).

Protecting the Family

As I have watched birds this spring and summer, I have noticed on several occasions smaller birds, like mockingbirds, chase larger birds, like hawks. How could the smaller birds ever expect to win against such huge birds?

Do you know what the little birds were doing? Protecting their young, their family. That's what a parent is all about, protecting the family from those giant forces that would destroy the family.

In our culture, those giants include drug and alcohol abuse, pornography, selfishness, and materialism, to name a few.

You can be assured that every day the big birds are out there trying to destroy your family. We must devote our time and energy to protecting the family. Those small birds provide a good model. When I saw them, the large birds were in retreat.

We will fight the giants. Make this a family day.

June 3

For example, when a woman marries, the law binds her to her husband as long as he is alive. But if he dies, the laws of marriage no longer apply to her (Romans 7:2, NLT).

June Weddings

June is wedding month – many people are committing their lives to each other for better or for worse until death do us part.

"Until death do us part" is not taken as seriously as it once was, but it needs to be. It would mean happier and stronger families.

Relationships in the younger years tend to concentrate on externals, good looks and popularity. But a little later, priorities change. You are looking for someone who is stable, a good parent, and a caring partner. Even someone "until death do us part."

June may be wedding month, but marriage is nothing to rush into. Good mate selection will mean the difference between joy and sorrow, happiness and misery over the long haul. Think about "until death do us part," and remember there are no limits to caring for your marriage.

June 4

He fell to the ground at Jesus' feet, thanking him for what he had done. This man was a Samaritan (Luke 17:9, NLT).

Prescription That Works

Once, there was a wise country doctor who prescribed what he called the "Thank-You Cure" for his patients. He realized that his patients were often burdened with the troubles of the world. As a result, they would come to him with symptoms of worry, stress, discouragement, and fear.

He would tell these patients to express appreciation to their family, friends, and everyone else they bumped into. As you might have guessed, many of the patients really started to feel better – just because they learned to say "thank you."

And you know, a "thank you" always requires a smile in order to get it just right.

Be thankful, always smile, count your blessings; as a matter of fact, do a recount daily, and you will find more blessings than you knew. That's a great fashion statement. Being thankful is a key to happiness. Count your blessings.

June 5

You had compassion on those in prison, and you joyfully accepted the plundering of your property since you knew that you yourselves had a better possession and an abiding one (Hebrews 10:34, ESV).

Compassion

This month, we will focus on Fathers. With the passing of my daddy several years ago, I want to reflect on his teachings. Daddy taught me compassion. We really were poor growing up. I didn't know it; it didn't matter.

Even under those circumstances, I learned compassion for those less fortunate than we were. Daddy didn't teach me a lesson about compassion; he just lived it. And all three of his children have a strong desire to help others. Daddy would always pick up people. He would always give them money if he thought they needed it.

Even in his last days, I was horrified that a homeless woman traveling along the road, who stopped in at a Wednesday night church service, ended up going home with them and spending the night. This background led me to understand that God had given me the gift of compassion that led me to be a part of VOA.

Daddy taught me compassion not by words but by what I saw.

June 6

For God so loved the world that he gave his only Son, that whoever believes in him should not perish but have eternal life (John 3:16, ESV).

Love is Action

One afternoon, Mary took her two children to the mall. When they arrived, they found a petting zoo. The kids begged to go. So Mary gave them a dollar each and watched as they ran toward the animals.

As Mary headed off to do some shopping, she saw her daughter coming behind her. Alarmed, she bent down and said, "What's wrong?"

Her daughter looked up and sadly said, "The petting zoo cost 2 dollars, so I gave Brandon my dollar." She had given her brother her dollar, even though no one loved cuddly furry creatures more than she.

So, Mary took her daughter back to the petting zoo, and together, they stood by the fence and watched Brandon as he petted and fed the animals.

That day Mary's daughter learned that love is action. But love is more…love is sacrificial action. Love always costs. Love gives; it doesn't grab. There are no limits to caring.

June 7

No soldier gets entangled in civilian pursuits since his aim is to please the one who enlisted him (2 Timothy 2:4, ESV).

Fish Out of Water

A research team was working off the coast of South Africa's Seal Island following shark activities. Suddenly, a great white shark jumped out of the water and landed in the boat.

Panicking, the shark thrashed about, cutting fuel lines and damaging equipment, not to mention terrifying the crew.

The shark's frantic behavior caused it to become entangled, trapping itself on the boat. The crew was unable to remove the shark. Throughout their efforts to return the terrifying predator back to the water, they kept it alive by splashing water on its gills so it could breathe.

The boat had to be towed to the harbor so the shark could be removed with a crane and then placed back into the water.

Do you ever feel like a fish out of water? We have certainly found ourselves in unchartered waters. Don't panic. You'll only find yourself more entangled. Together, let us help one another.

June 8

Take delight in honoring each other (Romans 12:10, NLT).

Marriage Communication

When John's lawn mower broke and would no longer run, his wife kept asking him to get it fixed. But somehow, he always had something else to do…you know, playing on the computer…fishing…golfing.

Finally, John's wife thought of a clever way to make her point. When John arrived home one day, he found her sitting on the overgrown lawn, snipping away the tall grass with a tiny pair of scissors.

He watched her for a short time and then went into the house. A few minutes later, he came out again and handed his wife a toothbrush. "When you finish cutting the grass," he said, "you might as well sweep the driveway."

The doctors say John will walk again, but he will always have a limp.

Communication is probably the single most important part of marriage, yet it can be a challenge to communicate more effectively. Practice good communication today with your spouse.

June 9

He makes the body fit together perfectly. As each part does its own special work, it helps the other parts grow so that the whole body is healthy and growing and full of love (Ephesians 4:16, NLT).

Three Men

There were three men. The first man married a woman and told her to do all the housework. It took about three days, but he finally saw she was doing all her chores.

The second man married a woman and gave her instructions to do all the cleaning and cooking. By the third day, he saw his house was clean and dinner was on the table.

The third man married a woman and told her to do all the housework, yard work, and cooking. The first two days he didn't see anything.

But by the third day, some of the swelling had gone down and he could see out of his left eye. His arm healed enough that he could fix dinner and mow the lawn. But he still has pain when he sits down.

Relationships work best when people work together. Treat your spouse with respect, and your future will look bright.

June 10

But you, take courage! Do not let your hands be weak, for your work shall be rewarded (2 Chronicles 15:7, ESV).

Take a Swing

Eric was in his first Little League baseball game. It was his first time at bat, and because he was scared, he never took a swing at the ball. He struck out by doing nothing! The coach was angry and told Eric that the next time he went to bat, he had to keep his eye on the ball and swing the bat.

The next time he was at bat, he swung at all three pitches and missed. "It's okay!" said the coach. "Keep swinging and you will eventually hit the ball."

The next time Eric went to bat, he swung. This time his bat hit the ball. And it was a home run!

Hank Aaron struck out 1383 times, but he hit 755 home runs...the world's record.

Don't stay in the dugout of life. Swing the bat. It's okay if you strike out. Just don't give up. Failure is not final.

June 11

In their greed they will make up clever lies to get hold of your money (2 Peter 2:3, NLT).

Greed

After disasters, we've often seen price gouging. This is Greed. We see it in a crisis…people wanting more than their fair share. You learned at home, in kindergarten, and in church, "Don't be greedy, share!"

Greed is a huge problem in our country. When is enough enough?

Much of our economic turmoil has to do with greed. When people buy more than they can afford, that's greed. Wall Street is a greedy place. So is Main Street. Greed is making our country sick and weak.

It's time to stop thinking about what we want, or how to keep up with the Joneses, or feeling that we are entitled to all our dreams.
Wouldn't it be wonderful if we could remember what we learned in kindergarten? Don't be greedy.

Why not go a step further and share what you have with others? Give! It will make all the difference in you and in our country. Giving destroys greed.

June 12

A word fitly spoken is like apples of gold in a setting of silver (Proverbs 25:11, ESV).

The Wranglers

In the early 1900's, some of the most talented writers at the University of Wisconsin divided themselves into two groups. One group was composed only of men. They used harsh criticism of each other's work, thus calling themselves the Stranglers.

The second group was composed of only women. They operated differently, using positive criticism and encouragement of each other's work. They called themselves the Wranglers.

Twenty years later, none of the Stranglers had been able to find success in literary careers. But several of the Wranglers had. Marjorie Rawlings, a Wrangler, had won a Pulitzer Prize for her novel, *The Yearling*.

Many things contribute to success, like hard work and dedication. But encouragement and support builds confidence and inspires others to keep going.

Positive words are powerful. Whether it's your child or your spouse, someone is listening to you. Make sure your words don't strangle.

June 13

Creation itself will be set free from its bondage to corruption and obtain the freedom of the glory of the children of God (Romans 8:21, ESV).

Untangled

A female humpback whale was found in the waters near San Francisco. She had become entangled in hundreds of crab traps and lines. The traps weighed her down, causing her to struggle to stay afloat. And the lines had wrapped around her body, tugging at her.

A rescue team arrived and decided that the only way to save her was to dive in and untangle her. They worked for hours, cutting each and every line, eventually freeing her.

When she was freed, the divers said the whale swam in what seemed like joyous circles. She then came back to each and every diver, one at a time, and nudged them as if thanking them.

Life can sometimes drag us down – get us entangled in tough issues. We all need people around us, friends and loved ones, who are willing to jump in and help us get untangled. A friend like that truly knows that there are no limits to caring.

June 14

Go to the ant, O sluggard; consider her ways, and be wise (Proverbs 6:6, ESV).

Unemployed Leno

Have you been unemployed? I remember when Jay Leno started his new job after being unemployed from his late-night show. From his own experience, he has tips for people in the job market.

First, be persistent. Do whatever it takes. Work hard! Jay once went to a car wash looking for a job. They didn't hire him. So the next morning, he returned and started washing cars. After three days of washing cars, the boss was so impressed he hired Jay.

Secondly, save your money. As a kid, Jay had two jobs…one at a car dealership and one at McDonald's. He would use the pay from one job for his bills. The pay from the second job was for savings. And for his entire life, he saved the money from one job and lived off the money from his second job.

Save your money. Be persistent, even if it is washing cars. Doors will open.

June 15

Let us lay aside every weight and sin which clings so closely, and let us run with endurance the race that is set before us (Hebrews 12:1, ESV).

Thomas Mitchell

Many of the earliest Australian explorers were convinced that they would come upon large river systems or even an inland sea. So they would often take boats with them.

Thomas Mitchell explored immense tracts of land throughout Australia in the early 1800s. While on his expeditions, he dragged two wooden boats over three thousand miles of dry land without once coming across any water. But he refused to leave them behind.

Even after his third expedition, he wrote that, although carrying the boats had been a great hindrance to his team, he was still unwilling to leave the boats behind.

Sometimes we hang on to things that only slow us down. We carry a load…perhaps from the past… that we don't need. Let go of the things that weigh you down…then you can face the challenges that lie ahead. What's your load? Let it go today. And leave it behind.

June 16

Bear one another's burdens, and so fulfill the law of Christ (Galatians 6:2, ESV).

Ralph

Ralph has sensitive skin that burns easily when exposed to the sun or the cold. He avoids the sunlight during the day and chilly evenings during the winter, staying indoors. Self-conscious about his appearance, he still hoped to get married one day.

He did…and she didn't mind his appearance either. Now he has a wife and two children, but he has to stay indoors and miss out on spending time with his family.

So a group of people decided to help Ralph by making a special wetsuit for him so he can enjoy the outdoors.

Ralph is a penguin. For unknown reasons, he loses his feathers every year, leaving his sensitive skin exposed. But thanks to workers at the wildlife center where he lives, Ralph can now spend more time enjoying the outdoors with his family and friends.

Surround yourself with loved ones who accept you no matter what and help you through life's difficult situations.

June 17

For though we live in the world, we do not wage war as the world does (2 Corinthians 10:3, NIV).

What's Next

We are experiencing turmoil in our country like we have never seen in the history of this nation. Everything has seemingly been forever changed. Our sense of security has been forever shaken. There was a time when from sea to shining sea, was the bosom of security. By and large, we were a united nation. Now we wonder.

What's next? A major war? Will we be great as always? Can this generation step up to the plate and be a part of the greatest generation that ever lived? The verdict is out.

We will answer that question from day to day. And the way we answer it will determine the future of our nation. The answer will have everything to do with core values that have made us a great country.

Freedom, justice, democracy --not just for a few but for all people.

This week, spend time with your family, express your love. Go to your house of worship, pray and give thanks.

We shall be ready for this test of time.

June 18

Not that I have already obtained this or am already perfect, but I press on to make it my own, because Christ Jesus has made me his own (Philippians 3:12, ESV).

Mr. Rogers

In Fred Roger's book, "The World According to Mr. Rogers," he shares a story about an apprentice carpenter.

The apprentice applied to a veteran master carpenter for a position on the older man's crew. As the master interviewed and questioned the young worker about his experience, the apprentice's pride was visible. He relayed how he had done this and that perfectly.

Finally, the older man asked whether the apprentice had ever made a mistake. Proudly, the younger man answered that indeed he had not. He waited patiently for the job offer he was sure to come, but it never did.

The older carpenter explained to the young man that when he did make a mistake, he wouldn't know how to fix it, having never made a mistake before.

Mr. Roger's story teaches the value of getting things wrong as well as right. It's only through experiencing mistakes that we learn how to handle them.

June 19

Train up a child in the way he should go; even when he is old he will not depart from it (Proverbs 22:6, ESV).

Roots and Wings

I have a riddle. What do roots and wings have in common?
Roots
- Will hold a giant oak tree in place for hundreds of years—through difficult storms.
- Give nourishment.
- Without the roots, there is no life.

On the other hand, wings
- Enable the giant eagle to sail high.
- Soar through the sky…
- Out of its nest to a new life.

Roots and Wings—what do they have in common? That's what every parent should give to his kids.
Roots
- Values that give stability
- Honesty, integrity,
- Commitment
- Staying the course through the storms—through the difficult times.

And Wings
- To leave the nest
- To create a life of their own
- To soar to new heights,
- To achieve the unthinkable.

That's our job as parents, and it's not over when they are 21—it's a lifetime commitment—roots and wings.

June 20

I have no greater joy than to hear that my children are walking in truth (3 John 1:4, NIV).

Ultimate Gift for Dad

The newspaper USA Today did an article on the "Ultimate Father's Day Gift." Do you have a clue what it is? – A Bugatti car.

This car goes zero to sixty in 2.5 seconds. It costs $1.5 million. It is basically the Godzilla of sports cars. Well, I didn't get one…none of the kids came through. I wasn't too disappointed. What would be that ultimate Father's Day gift for you?

For me, it would be that my children would love me in spite of my shortcomings. They would forgive me for my mistakes and remember the things I did right.

They would live out the values that I taught them – love, compassion, caring, hard work, a good family person.

Perhaps the ultimate gift to give is the reality that there are no limits to caring.

June 21

From the fig tree learn its lesson: as soon as its branch becomes tender and puts out its leaves, you know that summer is near (Mark 13:28, NLT).

Summer

Today starts the official first day of summer. This is the time of year many look forward to. The warmer weather, picnics, beach, skiing, fishing, a vacation, enjoying the flowers – taking it all in. At least that's our plans!

Well, today is the day to capture the moment. Take time to stop and smell the freshly bloomed flowers. Spend time with your children flying a kite. Appreciate the beauty all around you.

A friend forgot a lunch appointment. He spontaneously spent the day with his young son. And that father will never regret that day. And his son will never forget that day.

When you were young, what meant most to you? Playing, friends and having a good time! Be a child again and enjoy the summer. Spend time with friends and family and live life!

Relax, enjoy the day.

June 22

Every tithe of the land, whether of the seed of the land or of the fruit of the trees, is the LORD's; it is holy to the LORD (Leviticus 27:30, ESV).

Kurt Wagner

Kurt Warner was an average struggling father, working as a bag boy at a supermarket. However, he walked on for the St. Louis Rams NFL football team, and his life changed. A few years ago, in Atlanta, he was the quarterback who won the Super Bowl. What a change!

What hasn't changed, however, are his values and beliefs. He is a devout Christian who remains true to his convictions. One of his values involves giving. As a Christian, he gives 10% of his income to the church. After signing one of the largest contracts in NFL history, $47 million, he and his wife said, "We can't wait until we write our first tithe check to the church."

Kurt Warner has never forgotten the blessings of giving. Whether you hit it big or small, you can give. When we know the values of giving from the small amount, we will have the opportunity to give from the abundance.

June 23

Let your light shine before others so that they may see your good works and give glory to your Father who is in heaven (Matthew 5:16, ESV).

Not Looking

This is a child's perspective:

"When you thought I wasn't looking, I saw you hang my first painting on the refrigerator, and I immediately wanted to paint another one.

When you thought I wasn't looking, I saw you feed a stray cat, and I learned it was good to be kind to animals.

When you thought I wasn't looking, I saw you make my favorite cake for me, and I learned that little things can be the special things in life.

When you thought I wasn't looking, I heard you say a prayer, and I knew there is a God I could always talk to, and I learned to trust in God.

When you thought I wasn't looking, I saw you make a meal and take it to a friend who was sick, and I learned we all have to help take care of each other."

When you thought I wasn't looking, I saw by your actions there are no limits to caring.

June 24

You are to love those who are foreigners (Deuteronomy 10:10, NIV).

Lost in NYC

Mr. Mootoo, a native of South America, was visiting his brother in Queens, New York, when he decided to go for an afternoon stroll.

He quickly became disoriented and was found five days later when a couple saw him shivering in the cold. When they bought him a sandwich and offered to help him, Mr. Mootoo opened up and told them his story.

He later told authorities that he didn't ask for directions because he had heard scary things about New York and was afraid he'd be deported. He was too ashamed and shy to ask for food or directions. He had slept in an abandoned car while temperatures dropped into the 20's at night.

As for the couple who stopped to help? They told authorities, "When we see people in need, we try to help them."

We don't always need to know why people are in certain circumstances. All we have to do is to help them.

June 25

The LORD our God is providing you a place of rest
(Joshua 1:13, ESV).

Mayberry

I sure would like to go to Mayberry. Have you ever been? I've seen it on television – I've always wanted to go to Mayberry.

Sit on Andy's porch after supper, get a haircut at Floyd's, get Gomer to fill up my car with gas, and check the oil. Maybe go down to the lake.

Don't have to worry about crime with Andy and Barney on duty. I've always wanted to go to Mayberry.

But I've discovered that Mayberry is only in one's mind. We long for the good ole days – less stress, less fear, less hassle. But the good old days like Mayberry are just in our minds.

Even the people at Mayberry longed for the good ole days.

However, you can choose to slow down – take a few minutes to escape to your own Mayberry. Find peace, be kind, offer help, don't drive fast, pick up after yourself, sit on your porch and relax. That's Mayberry!

June 26

He has not ignored or belittled the suffering of the needy. He has not turned his back on them but has listened to their cries for help (Psalm 22:24, NLT).

Get Involved

A man was walking home late one evening when he heard screams coming from behind a clump of bushes. He was hearing the sounds of a struggle. A woman was being attacked.

The man hesitated, uncertain if he should get involved. Perhaps he should go get help. But he had to act…and fast.

He ran behind the bushes and pulled the attacker off the woman. They struggled for a few moments until the attacker ran away.

The rescuer approached the girl, who was crouched behind a tree, sobbing. Trying to comfort her he said, "It's safe now. The man ran away."

After a long pause, the girl said, "Dad, is that you?" Looking closer through the shadows, the man realized the girl he rescued was his daughter. Every day, we have opportunities to help others. Whether it's a simple act of kindness or even a chance to save a life. It could be someone you love.

There are no limits to caring ®

June 27

Gray hair is a crown of glory (Proverbs 16:31, ESV).

Never Too Old

Anthony Smith, an 85-year-old British sailor, finally fulfilled his lifelong dream of crossing the Atlantic on a raft. The 2,800-mile crossing took about two months and he brought 3 of his close friends with him.

The men wanted to raise money for a nonprofit group that provides drinking water to impoverished communities. And they also wanted to prove the elderly are capable of adventures. Think of the great men and women who continued to pursue their dreams into old age.

1. Moses, at 80 years old, led 3.5 million people out of captivity
2. Colonel Sanders, at 70, discovered "finger-lickin' good" chicken
3. Picasso was painting at 88
4. Thomas Edison invented the mimeograph machine at 85
5. John Wesley was still traveling on horseback and preaching at 85
6. Ronald Regan was 70 when he began his first term as president.
7. Joe Biden became president at the age of 78!

Don't let your age dictate what you achieve today.

June 28

Be joyful in hope, patient in affliction, faithful in prayer
(Romans 12:12, NIV).

Victor Villasenor

Victor Villaseñor (Vee ya sen your) was illiterate because of dyslexia until adulthood. When he did learn to read, he decided he wanted to become a writer, and he asked God to help him.

He worked as a laborer, digging ditches and cleaning houses. His mind was free to think and dream up stories. At home, he read books, analyzed writing styles, and began writing.

He wrote 9 novels, 65 stories, and 10 plays. He sent them to publishers. All were rejected.

Then in 1972, after 260 rejections, Villaseñor sold his first novel, called *Macho*. He then published a nonfiction and a screenplay.

His crowning work was a novel about his family called *Rain of Gold* that took him twelve years to write. With a lot of hard work on Villaseñor's part, God answered his prayer. When we have a passion and a prayer, we must be dedicated to put forth the hard work and perseverance to see the blessings.

There are no limits to caring ®

June 29

Behold, one shall fly swiftly like an eagle (Jeremiah 48:40, ESV).

Flying Above the Storm

Did you know that an eagle is aware that a storm is approaching long before it arrives? The eagle will fly to a high spot and wait for the winds to come. When the storm hits, the eagle will set its wings so that the wind will pick it up and lift it high above the storm.

As the storm rages, the eagle is soaring high above it, gliding with ease. The eagle doesn't escape the storm; it simply uses the storm to lift it higher.

When the storms come, we can allow the winds to lift us or sink us. But we can't escape the storm.

Remember, it is not the burdens of life that weigh us down, but it is how we handle them that counts.

Be an eagle. Let God's winds lift you above the burdens of this day. Soar to new heights. Fly above the storms. See the beauty!

June 30

Don't be selfish; don't try to impress others. Be humble, thinking of others as better than yourselves (Philippians 2:3, NLT).

Michael Phelps

Michael Phelps won the most Olympic gold medals at a single event, eight gold medals. In addition, he holds seven world records.

But as much as he is motivated to win in the 2004 Olympic swim meet in Athens, he suppressed his competitive nature and gave up his spot for a gold medal.

Phelps had already won several gold medals in Athens, but his teammate, Ian Crocker, had not. So, Phelps deferred his turn on the butterfly race. Because of that, Ian Crocker won the gold for that event…a gold that Phelps could have won easily.

Phelps said, "I'm proud of giving someone like Ian a chance. That was very exciting."

Phelps wanted to win the gold at every opportunity. But he became a bigger winner when gave his opportunity to Crocker to win a gold medal.

Be willing to sacrifice so that others can also realize their dreams.

July 1

Study this Book of instruction continually. Meditate on it day and night so you will be sure to obey everything written in it. Only then will you prosper and succeed in all you do (Joshua 1:8, NLT).

Formulas for Success

Jim Rohn says, "Success is neither magical nor mysterious. Success is the natural consequence of consistently applying basic fundamentals." Two outstanding coaches offered fundamentals for success.

Coach Lou Holtz gives a formula for success consisting of three rules:
1. "Do what's right. Be on time, be polite and be honest; remain free from drugs and if you have any questions, get out your Bible.
2. Do your best. Mediocrity is unacceptable when you are capable of doing better.
3. Treat others as you want to be treated. Practice love and understanding."

Bear Bryant said, "Show class, have pride, and display character. If you do, winning takes care of itself."

Those are some fundamentals from two men who knew what it takes to win in life. They are not magical ways; they are proven ways to produce great results.

July 2

As the Lord has forgiven you, so you also must forgive (Colossians 3:13, ESV).

Louis Zamperini

Young Louis Zamperini was always in trouble. But his brother saw the good in him and helped convert his negative self-image to a winner in long-distance running.

He became the fastest high school runner in the country and then went on to run in the 1936 Olympics in Berlin. Later, Zamperini joined the army to fight in World War II.

His plane crash-landed, killing part of the crew. He survived 47 days at sea, and while he was on the small raft at sea, he found faith in God. He was captured by the Japanese and treated with horrific cruelty—unbelievable.

But when he got home after two years in captivity, he learned that the only way to deal with his past was through forgiveness. He went back, met with those who tortured him, and forgave them. On this day in 2014, Louis died at the age of 97. Forgiveness allows us to let go!

July 3

Who comforts us in all our affliction so that we may be able to comfort those who are in any affliction, with the comfort with which we ourselves are comforted by God (2 Corinthians 1:4, ESV).

Independence

Tomorrow is Independence Day! It is a time to remember our heritage and celebrate the unique freedoms we enjoy in these United States of America. But how do you celebrate freedom or independence?

Is it just a matter of taking a day off from work, shooting some fireworks, picnicking, or listening to patriotic music? None of those are bad activities, and a lot of that sort of thing will take place today.

Another way to celebrate independence is to engage in helping someone achieve independence. At VOA, we assist individuals to grow and develop to their fullest capacity.

We move people toward independence by helping them learn how to take care of themselves, earn an income, own a home, and in many other ways helping them realize more of the American dream.

You can reach out today and help someone toward greater independence with a hand-up or a word of encouragement.

July 4

For freedom Christ has set us free (Galatians 5:1, ESV).

Independence Day

Fifty-six men signed the Declaration of Independence. Of the 56 men,
- Five were captured by the British and tortured to death.
- Twelve had their homes burned.
- Two lost their sons in the War.
- Another had two sons captured.
- Nine of them fought and died during the war.
- Carter Braxton saw his ships sunk by the British navy. He died in poverty.
- Thomas Nelson's home was taken by British General Cornwallis.
- John Hart's home was raided by British forces. He fled for his life and sent his children into hiding. When he returned home, he found his wife dead, and his children vanished. He died shortly thereafter.

We celebrate Independence Day on the fourth of July. We celebrate our freedom. But as you can see, freedom isn't free.

July 5

Lay up for yourselves treasures in heaven, where neither moth nor rust destroys and where thieves do not break in and steal (Matthew 6:20, ESV).

Fireworks

I don't know about you, but I enjoy watching fireworks. There's something magical about those brilliant colors exploding against the dark sky. They are breathtaking and exciting to watch…but only for a moment. They don't last forever.

The same is true of many of the experiences in our lives. We fight and struggle for things that seem beautiful and alluring. They may seem wonderful at the moment, but they don't last…just like fireworks—a big glow—and then gone.

Maybe it's a shiny new car or speedboat. Maybe it's a big, impressive house. It might even be a promotion or a prestigious career. So many of the things of this world are like fireworks. They look great for a moment but don't last.

Why struggle for things that don't last? Instead, focus on the important things that never lose their value…freedom, independence, caring, giving, forgiving, and loving your neighbor or going the extra mile. There are no limits to caring.

July 6

What therefore God has joined together, let not man separate (Mark 10:9, ESV).

Mates for Life

From my back porch, I've been watching a pair of Canada geese. As a result of my interest, I have learned that Canadian geese mate for life. Once a mate is chosen, the couple remains together for the rest of their lives.

Isn't it interesting that Canadian geese provide a good lesson for us? Choosing a mate is a lifetime commitment, not a 90-day return option. Marriage is for life, and it is important to honor that commitment.

Obviously, there are events that keep commitment from being lived out. But for the sake of each other, mates must be chosen for life, not a 90-day trial or even a three-year lease.

Mates for life are about roots, and roots are what we need in a rootless society.

Consider the Canada geese. There are no limits to caring – even for a lifetime.

July 7

But you will receive power when the Holy Spirit has come upon you, and you will be my witnesses in Jerusalem and in all Judea and Samaria, and to the end of the earth
(Acts 1:8, ESV).

Reach Out

Sue loves dogs! Recently, on a mission trip, she saw many dogs roaming the streets, but they were street dogs... not wanting to be played with or hugged on. Their goal was to find food, water, and shelter from the sun.

In a similar way, we are surrounded by people searching for answers... trying to survive. They may need food, water, and shelter or may be searching to fill an emotional or spiritual void in their lives.

They need people like you and me who will give them food, water, and shelter. People to share God's message of salvation, hope, and freedom.

The Bible says, "Go into all the world and preach the gospel" and "Therefore, as we have opportunity, let us do good to all people."

NOW is the time to do what God has been calling you to do. Do something! Show love! Be kind! Give to others! Pray for others!

July 8

I believe that I shall look upon the goodness of the LORD in the land of the living (Psalm 27:13, ESV).

Rockefeller "I Believe"

We live in a strange world, and it seems like we lost our direction and values. John D. Rockefeller wrote "I believe" during some difficult times. And I was impressed with what I read. Listen:

I believe in the supreme worth of the individual and in his right to life, liberty, and the pursuit of happiness.

I believe that every right implies a responsibility; every opportunity, an obligation; every possession, a duty.

I believe that the law was made for humans and not humans for the law; that government is the servant of the people and not their master.

I believe in the dignity of labor, whether with head or hand, that the world owes no man a living but that it owes every man an opportunity to make a living.

I believe that thrift is essential to well-ordered living and that economy is a prime requisite of a sound financial structure, whether in government, business, or personal affairs. Sounds like what we need.

July 9

Jesus replied, "They do not need to go away. You give them something to eat" (Matthew 14:16, NIV).

Your Fish

Jesus had been teaching a large crowd, possibly 20,000 people. And Jesus asked...how are we going to feed all these people? (He already knew).

He says to Philip, "Where can we buy enough food for all these people...could you call in an order to Jason's Deli?" Philip said, "But how can we pay for it? It would take half a year's salary to give everyone just a bite."

Andrew spoke up, "There's a boy here who has a couple of fish and some bread." But as an afterthought Andrew said, "How many people would that feed?" Up to 20,000 people with 12 baskets left over...because the boy gave it to Jesus.

What would you have done with your fish?

What if all the elderly people in our community had enough to eat tonight? What if 26% of children in Alabama who live in poverty had enough to eat...they could if you gave your fish.

July 10

He lifted me out of the slimy pit, out of the mud and mire; he set my feet on a rock and gave me a firm place to stand. He put a new song in my mouth (Psalm 40:2-3, NIV).

Tragedy into Triumph

During this uncertain economic time, don't let difficulties defeat you. You can turn tragedy into triumph.

J.K. Rowling was fired from her job as a secretary. She decided to use her free time to write books... Harry Potter books. She is now one of the most successful women in Britain.

Mary Kay Ash was a single mom forced into early retirement with only a small amount in savings. She took that savings and opened a cosmetics store, hiring door-to-door "beauty consultants." Today, Mary Kay brings in over $1 billion a year, with sales reps around the world.

When *Look* magazine closed in the 70s, Pat Mitchell lost her job. She decided to pursue a career in television. Over the next 30 years, she became a successful producer, and in 2000, became president of PBS.

When you face tragedies, turn your misfortune into a new life. You can recover from life's challenging adversities.

July 11

Hear, O my people, while I admonish you! O Israel, if you would but listen to me! (Psalm 81:13, ESV).

Kind Edward

King Edward VII was enjoying lunch with his family when suddenly the King's grandson yelled, "Grandpa!"

Gently but firmly, King Edward turned to his grandson and told the young boy that he must not interrupt while adults are talking. But a moment later, his grandson yelled out again, "But Grandpa, grandpa!"

The King remained patient and told him again, "You must not speak while I'm speaking. When I have finished speaking, then you will be allowed to talk."

A little while later, King Edward turned back to his grandson and said kindly, "Now I've finished talking. What was it that you wanted to say?" His grandson replied, "I was going to tell you there was a caterpillar on your lettuce, but it's all right, you've eaten it.'"

Never get too busy to listen to your family, your spouse, and your children. They have something important to tell you. What is it?

July 12

Those who lead blameless lives and do what is right, speaking the truth from sincere hearts (Psalm 15:2, NLT).

All Wet

A young boy was forbidden to go swimming in the lake near his house. One day he arrived home with his hair all wet. His mother demanded an explanation.

"I fell in the lake," he said. "Well, why aren't your clothes wet?" his mother asked.

"Because I had a feeling I was going to fall in and I took them off." Some excuses sound thinner than others, but that one was all wet! His mom had a painful remedy for that kind of storytelling.

There's really no substitute for telling the truth. When you tell the truth, you don't have to struggle to remember what you said the last time you told your story because it never changes. That takes a lot of pressure off and makes for much better relationships. Honesty is always the best policy. Otherwise, you eventually come out looking all wet!

July 13

May the LORD smile down on you and show you his kindness (Numbers 6:25, ERV).

Smile

Someone has said, "Of all the things you wear, your expression is the most important."

Mother Teresa said, "Every time you smile at someone, it is an action of love, a gift to that person, a beautiful thing."

Just think, your smile is an action of love…like Mother Teresa!

When someone smiles at you, doesn't it usually cause you to receive them well? And doesn't a frown on another person's face bring you down just a bit? Just think, today, your smile could be the brightest part of someone's life…an act of love.

During these economic times, you may not be able to give as you have in the past. But how much does it cost to smile? That's a no-cost gift. Smile today, and the world will smile with you. And you will share a face of love… Mother Teresa.

Have a great day smiling – a gift of love.

July 14

One generation commends your works to another; they tell of your mighty acts (Psalms 145:4, NIV).

The Handoff

In the Olympic Games, the American team in the track and field relay race lost the race because of a bad handoff. Actually, both the men's and women's teams lost the gold because they dropped the batons.

We can have the fastest runners in the world, but the race is always won or lost in the handoff. USA Track and Field president Doug Logan vowed future American athletics teams will be better. Logan stated, "Ultimately, the athletes on the track are the only ones who can successfully pass the stick around the track, but they need proper leadership and preparation."

As in our own lives, we must pass the baton successfully to the next generation. The baton of patriotism, work ethic, family values, love, compassion, giving, and sharing…we must not drop the baton in the handoff…our children are counting on winning the race. They need leadership and preparation. Now is the time.

July 15

Please test your servants for ten days: Give us nothing but vegetables to eat (Daniel 1:12, NIV).

Green Garden

Wayne was a carpenter and had been out of work for two years. Living with his family, they had little income. Wayne planted a garden in his backyard, growing his own vegetables to reduce the cost of groceries.

One morning, he was digging in his garden, looking for broccoli, when he discovered something buried in the dirt. He kept digging and pulled out a bag filled with $150,000.

Although it wasn't the green that he had expected to find while digging in his garden, he definitely found a treasure.

Growing a garden and eating healthy has benefits. And while you probably won't find hidden treasures in your back yard, you will reap other rewards of a nutritious diet.

Eating fruits, vegetables, and fish can pay off in the long run…saving you thousands of dollars in doctor visits and medications. Good health and a long life…now that's a treasure.

July 16

Get up, for it is your duty to tell us how to proceed in setting things straight (Ezra 10:4, NLT).

Who Speaks for You

Several men are in the locker room after exercising when a cell phone on one of the benches rings. A man answers, "Hello?" The woman on the phone says, "Honey, I'm at the mall and saw this beautiful mink coat. Can I buy it?" "Yes," the man answers.

"I also stopped by the Mercedes dealership and found a brand-new model at a great price, only $90,000. Can I go ahead and get it?" "Okay," the man answered. The woman said, "Thank you so much! I love you!" The man hangs up and asks, "Whose phone is this?"

Sometimes others speak for us when we may not want them to. The adult child whose parent still speaks for them… the woman whose husband always nominates her for everything.

Sometimes we allow others to speak for us when we should speak for ourselves. Who makes your commitments? Perhaps it's time to take charge of your own phone and commitments because they are important when it's time to pay the bill.

There are no limits to caring ®

July 17

Abide in me, and I in you (John 15:4, ESV).

Sync

Have you synced up today? You know …with your computers, cell phones, mp3 players, and other electronic devices. When synced, linked together, technology can function at its very best.

But a better question for today…have you allowed God to sync His life with you? When we are synced up with God, we will be our very best.

How do we do that? First, we must submit our life to him…linking up. Second, we must spend time with Him, synching our lives with who He is. Third, we must listen as he speaks to us and orchestrates our lives.

What then? If we are synced with Him, we will hear Him when he tells us to speak a kind word to the cashier, cut our neighbor's grass because they've been sick, or donate time or money to help those in need.

Jesus said, "Abide with me and I in you." That's syncing with God.

July 18

Giving a gift can open doors; it gives access to important people (Proverbs 18:16, NLT).

Giving Two

Winston Churchill said, "We make a living by what we get, but we make a life by what we give." What in your life are you giving, and to whom are you giving it? To your family? To your loved ones? To people you don't know? To people in need?

Dr. Douglas Lawson has written a book entitled *101 WAYS YOU CAN IMPROVE THE WORLD AND YOUR LIFE*. In it, he describes dozens of physical, mental, and spiritual benefits which occur as a direct result of giving our time, energy, money, and service to others. Giving is healthy.

Life is not about what you take or what you get, but it has everything to do with what you give. There is real joy in giving and sharing with other people, and if you have found that ability to give and to share, you have found joy in living.

July 19

Your beauty should not come from outward adornment . . . rather, it should be that of your inner self, the unfading beauty of a gentle and quiet spirit (1 Peter 3:3-4, NIV).

Olympic Beauty

In the Beijing Olympics opening ceremony, a cute Chinese girl mouthed the words to "Ode to the Motherland" …while the real singer was behind the stage. According to the music director, she wasn't "good looking enough for the ceremony."

One girl had the voice…the other had the looks. Officials said that it was an attempt to represent the best of China in the Beijing Olympics.

It's hard for us to imagine such a thing in America…but is it really so different here?

Could we be guilty of something similar? We tell girls that they aren't skinny enough. They should dress a certain way, wear makeup, have plastic surgery…so that they can be beautiful.

We have always been taught that beauty is on the inside…not on the outside. We need to readjust our focus to that true inner beauty – one's gifts and talents, not the package that they are wrapped in.

July 20

For the righteous falls seven times and rises again
(Proverbs 24:16, ESV).

Shove

A little girl, dressed in her Sunday best, was running fast, trying not to be late for Bible class. As she ran she prayed, "Dear Lord, please don't let me be late!... please don't let me be late!"

As she ran, she tripped over a curb and fell, getting her clothes dirty. She got up, brushed herself off, and started running. She once again began to pray, "Dear Lord, please don't let me be late!... and don't shove me down again!"

Sometimes when trying to do the right thing, we take a spill. We feel like we have been treated unjustly or unfairly. It's like God, or fate, or something has tripped us up.

The truth is, if we attempt to do anything significant in life, there will be times when we stumble and fall. When it happens to us, like the little girl, we need to get up, keep on running, and keep on praying.

There are no limits to caring ®

July 21

The two shall become one flesh. So they are no longer two but one flesh (Mark 10:8, ESV).

Thunderstorms

One summer evening, during a violent thunderstorm, a mother was tucking her small boy into bed. She was about to turn off the light when he asked with a tremor in his voice, "Mommy, will you sleep with me tonight?" The mother smiled and gave him a reassuring hug. "I can't dear," she said, "I have to sleep with Daddy."

A long silence was broken, at last by a shaken little voice saying, "The big sissy."

Though the storms may rage outside, the family is much stronger when the spouse is the main focus. Remind your husband or wife – today- that he/she is the most important person in your life.

And parents, the best gift you can give your children is to let them know how much you love your spouse, the number 1 person in your life. "For this cause shall a man leave his father and mother and cleave to his wife."

July 22

An excellent wife who can find? She is far more precious than jewels (Proverbs 31:10, ESV).

Fleming's Suit

Sir Sandford Fleming was a Canadian engineer who created the worldwide time zones. A brilliant man.

When he was dating his future wife, he chose a nice fabric and had his tailor make him a new suit.

The next morning, Fleming wore his new suit traveling to visit his fiancé. On his way, he noticed that everyone he passed on the street seemed to be very amused and jovial. Fleming was delighted by everyone's good mood.

But his amusement quickly left him when his fiancé answered his knock at the door, and she too began roaring with laughter.

The cause of everyone's amusement was Fleming's new suit. Being colorblind, he had unknowingly chosen a pale pink fabric for his suit. From then on, his future wife vowed to help him choose his clothes.

You may be brilliant, but a good spouse can help you with your weaknesses and love you in spite of them. Be open… Be loved.

July 23

Greet the friends, each by name (3 John 15, ESV).

Facebook

Listen to what someone gave me. I am trying to make friends outside of Facebook while applying the same principles.

Therefore, every day I walk down the street and tell passers-by what I have eaten, how I feel at the moment, what I have done the night before, what I will do later, and with whom.

I give them pictures of my family, my dog, and of me gardening, taking things apart in the garage, watering the lawn, standing in front of landmarks, driving around town, having lunch, and doing what anybody and everybody does every day.

I also listen to their conversations, give them a "thumbs up," and tell them I like them. And it works just like Facebook! I already have four people following me: two police officers, a private investigator, and a psychiatrist.

Wow! Facebook, cell phones, etc…Are we really more intimate? Maybe we should just try old fashion friendship…come and see me…let's talk!

July 24

But solid food is for the mature, for those who have their powers of discernment trained by constant practice to distinguish good from evil (Hebrews 5:14, ESV).

Bigger

Our three-year-old granddaughter, Kayden, was so excited about her birthday. On this day she was three years old, but tomorrow she would be four! The next day I said, "Kayden, You're four. How do you like that?" She says, "Yes, but I'm not any bigger." She was just a little disappointed. Expected to be bigger!

Sometimes I'm disappointed that I am not any bigger than I was when I was three. Big enough to share… big enough to forgive… to let go. Big enough to give… big enough to ignore someone who does me wrong. How big am I anyway?

The real test in life is not how big you are but how mature you are. Maturity is the furthest distance from infancy. Sometimes it seems like we get stuck in infancy.

May we grow, be all we can be, and learn what counts. It's not about me. It's really about others.

July 25

Whoever brings blessing will be enriched (Proverbs 11:25, ESV).

Self-Esteem

Self-esteem is the value or worth we place upon ourselves. It is how we see ourselves and has everything to do with how we live, how we behave, and what we do in life.

Our behavior reinforces our self-esteem, which is why good behavior is important. Good behavior generates good self-esteem, and bad behavior generates poor self-esteem.

If we want to enhance our self-esteem, we need to reach out to people in need and give of ourselves, our time, and energy. That not only blesses someone else, but it helps our self-esteem because we find true worth and value in life. Feeling good about oneself makes it easier to meet the challenges of life and to make the right decisions.

If you want to improve your self-concept, help somebody else today. Not only will their value increase, but yours will too.

July 26

Repeat them again and again to your children. Talk about them when you are at home and when you are on the road, when you are going to bed and when you are getting up (Deuteronomy 6:7, NLT).

Technology

Wash your hands! Turn off the water!! Flush the toilet!! Turn off the lights! Close the doors!

These were things I heard and learned growing up. I have those tapes deep within my psychic. And they are easily replayed. But I have a problem with these tapes! Technology has made some of these teachings obsolete!

When I go into a bathroom now at the airport, the water comes on and goes off by itself. The toilets flush with no help from me!! But when I go home, the technology is not there. Back to the olden days. You flush it yourself.

Our challenge is to teach our kids values that transcend time and technology. Like, "I am responsible for myself and my messes. I need to be a good steward of what has been entrusted to me."

A child learns more by what we do…than by what we say. We are role models! Sometimes good ones, and sometimes we need improvement.

July 27

It is more blessed to give than to receive (Acts 20:35, ESV).

Givers and Takers

There are two basic types of people, the takers and the givers.

Booker T. Washington said, "The happiest are those who do the most for others." Winston Churchill said, "We make a living by what we get, but we make a life by what we give."

Jesus said, "It is more blessed to give than to receive."

In Israel, there is a body of water called the Dead Sea. It is called the Dead Sea because it only receives water and holds it. Nothing flows from it. The name is appropriate, for something that does not give is truly dead.

Your life can be a dead sea, or it can be a sea of living water to other people. That is the choice we make every day. We can become a spring of living water to a thirsty world.

To be a giver or a taker. That one decision will make all the difference in your life.

July 28

You shall follow my rules and keep my statutes and walk in them. I am the LORD your God (Leviticus 18:4, ESV).

Playing Checkers

Have you ever played a game with someone who did not know the rules of the game? You think they know how to play, and in the middle of the game, you suddenly realize they don't have a clue.

Recently I was playing checkers with a family friend who indicated that she knew all the rules. Halfway through the game, I realized she didn't have a clue. She didn't know what a king was. Dead giveaway.

Sometimes in life, there are people who just don't know the rules of the game of life. They don't have a clue. The first rule is "Do unto others as you would have them do unto you." Halfway through life, I realize some don't know that fundamental rule.

But that rule comes alive in treating one another with kindness and compassion, with love and respect, with dignity and honor.

Another rule that we forget sometimes is there are no limits to caring. Live it.

July 29

May he grant you your heart's desire and fulfill all your plans! (Psalm 20:4, ESV).

Wilma Rudolph

Wilma Rudolph began life with a fight, being born weighing only four and a half pounds. At four years old, she contracted polio and lost the use of her left leg. She could have let her circumstances keep her down but instead, Wilma was determined and decided she wanted to do more.

She overcame her physical and emotional challenges and went on to win three Olympic gold medals in track and field. Wow! Instead of allowing her circumstances to decide how her life would be, she decided that she would fight for a better future…a better life.

Even after Wilma's athletic career and Olympic wins, she didn't stop there. She wanted to help others in their athletic pursuits. Through consulting, writing, and sports clinics, she continued to motivate and encourage others to pursue their dreams.

Whatever you're facing, find your motivation to accomplish your goals and dreams today.

July 30

*Watch out! Be on your guard against all kinds of greed;
life does not consist in an abundance of possessions*
(Luke 12:15, NIV).

Consumption

In this country, we are consuming more stuff than ever before. We are overeating, overdrinking, overspending…but does that bring us happiness or misery?

- Globally 20% of the world's richest countries are consuming 86% of total private consumption
- The richest 20% consumes 45% of all meat and fish. The poorest 20% consume less than 5%.
- The richest 20% consume 58% of total energy. The poorest 20% consume less than 4%.
- The richest 20% owns 87% of the world's vehicles, the poorest 20% less than 1%.

If happiness were based on consumption, we would be the happiest people in the world. But many in our country are not happy! Mother Teresa was poor, but she knew joy.

Consumption is a spiritual thing. It's not what you consume that produces joy. It's what you give.

July 31

To draw near to listen is better than to offer the sacrifice of fools (Ecclesiastes 5:1, ESV).

Dru Sweatman

Dru Sweatman is a mom, married to Morgan. They have a 10-year-old son Matt. Dru has never heard a word her husband has said or her son. She has been deaf since she was 5.

But all of that changed a few years ago. For the first time she heard her son say, "Mom." And her husband spoke, and she listened. What a miracle!

She had an implant, and it worked. What joy occurred in this home!

Do you hear the voice of your husband, your child, or your friend? What do you hear? Same ole thing? But if you had a miracle, you could hear as you have never heard before.

We have two ears for listening and one tongue for talking! But for most, the art of listening is as challenging as it was for Dru. But miracles do happen, even in your home. The miracle of hearing what others are saying. Do you hear me?

August 1

Your kindness will reward you (Proverbs 11:17, NLT).

Joe Torre

Sometime ago, Bill and I were trying to catch a cab. As I reached for the back door of the cab, I realized I was stepping ahead of a gentleman. I moved back and he said, "Going to the airport?" I replied, "Yes." He said, "Hop in."

Bill and I rode to the airport. Bill knew our host, Joe. They had met in Viet Nam. They recounted their visit to Viet Nam and a lot of baseball talk. When we got to the airport, Joe paid our cab fare and departed with warm goodbyes.

Bill said, "You don't know who he was?" So, who was this kind man? Joe Torre, now of the New York Yankees.

Four world championships later, I still remember this man for his kindness. He was an important person, but then, every person is important who is kind.

We may not be world known as Joe Torre, but each of us has the opportunity to be kind--and thus significant.

There are no limits to caring ®

August 2

And he awoke and rebuked the wind and said to the sea, "Peace! Be still!" And the wind ceased, and there was a great calm (Mark 4:39, ESV).

Picture of Peace

A king offered a prize to the artist who could paint the best picture of peace. When the King looked at all the pictures, there were two he really liked, and he had to choose between them.

One picture was of a calm lake. The lake was a perfect mirror with peaceful towering mountains all around it. Overhead was a blue sky with fluffy white clouds. Many thought this was the perfect picture of peace.

The other picture had rugged, bare mountains with a dark sky from which rain and lightning were seen. A waterfall tumbled down the mountain. When the King looked behind the waterfall, he saw a tiny bush growing in a crack in the rock where a mother bird had built her nest. There she sat in perfect peace.

The king chose the second picture. He said, "Peace means to be in the midst of difficult things and still be calm in your heart."

August 3

Prove me, O LORD, and try me; test my heart and my mind (Psalm 26:2, ESV).

Dale

How's your heart? Dale's heart is impacted by what he eats. The quality of his life will be determined by what he takes in. If he eats vegetables, fruits, and fish, his heart arteries likely will not clog up…after all, Dale will need his heart for the rest of his life…no exceptions.

There's another heart that works the same way. Our heart of compassion. If we see people as only statistics or if we walk by someone in the ditch, it may indicate that our heart is clogged up and needs a bypass…new arteries of love, not clogged up with self-centeredness.

What can make your heart better? Ironically, your physical heart is also helped by what you do with your emotional heart…studies show that you can have a healthier heart if you learn to give and care for one another. Giving is for the heart.

Eat healthily, give healthily, and find the fullness of a long life. There are no limits to caring. That's a good heart.

August 4

For by you I can run against a troop, and by my God I can leap over a wall (Psalm 18:29, ESV).

Komen Foundation

Suzy and Nancy were as close as two sisters can get. After college, Nancy moved away. Although separated by distance, they spoke every day by phone. One afternoon, Nancy received an especially important call. Suzy had been diagnosed with breast cancer.

After surgery, Suzy thought she was cured. But six months later, her cancer had spread. And she soon died. After Suzy's death, Nancy wanted to do something to honor the memory of her sister. But what difference could one person make?

Nancy founded the Susan G. Komen Foundation, which is one of the world's largest non-profits dedicated to the fight against breast cancer.

Out of this tragedy came a blessing to millions of women today who work to prevent breast cancer or find a cure.

August 5

He will not grow faint or be discouraged (Isaiah 42:4, ESV).

Discouraged

A father arrived at his son's little league baseball game shortly after the first inning had begun. He approached his son sitting on the bench behind the first baseline and asked what the score was.

"We're behind 12 to nothin'," he answered grinning ear to ear. "Really," the father replied, "You don't look very discouraged." "Discouraged?" the boy asked with a puzzled look on his face. "Why should we be discouraged? We haven't even been up to bat yet."

Sometimes in life, we feel like we are being dealt the "raw end of the deal," and we can't catch a break. We could learn a lot from the optimism of this little boy.

Perhaps you just haven't had your chance at-bat, or maybe you struck out.

In life, we can't predict what it will throw at us. Just be prepared to respond. Do your best. Stay positive, stay focused and be ready for any ball.

August 6

Be strong in the Lord and in his mighty power (Ephesians 6:10, NIV).

Strength

In your mind, visualize a giant bulldozer as it carves a path through tons of earth and rock. Now, shift your vision to that of a young mother's hands gently caressing her infant. Which is the picture of strength? The answer is that both are images of incredible strength.

Strength, like power, is always related to its usage. The brute force of a bulldozer can move a mountain. But the tender touch of a mother or father can provide security and peace for a child. Both kinds of strength are needed in our world.

We were never meant to be strong alone. Ephesians 6:10 says to "be strong in the Lord and in His mighty power." You don't have to have muscles to be strong. A helping hand, caring touch, or a word of encouragement can be powerful. You have the power to enable and draw out the strength in others.

August 7

Their weakness was turned to strength (Hebrews 11:34, NLT).

Tommy Cooper

Tommy Cooper discovered his unique gifts for entertaining at the age of 17, aspiring to be a great magician. But Tommy suffered from extreme stage fright.

As soon as he walked onto the stage, he forgot all his lines. Every magic trick he performed went terribly wrong. His grand finale was to fill a bottle with milk, then turn it over. The milk was supposed to stay in the bottle. But instead, the milk poured all over Tommy.

Mortified, he abruptly walked off the stage, believing himself to be a failure. That's when he heard the audience clapping and cheering…a standing ovation.

Tommy Cooper decided that his days as a magician were over. Instead, he became a great comedian.

Sometimes mishaps can create an opportunity to discover your potential. Don't cry over spilled milk. Today's misfortune could be tomorrow's blessings.

August 8

Let each of you look not only to his own interests, but also to the interests of others (Philippians 2:4, ESV).

Dentist

A man and his wife walked into a dentist's office.

The man says to the dentist, "I'm in one heck of a hurry; I have two buddies in my car waiting to go play golf, so forget about the anesthetic. I just want you to pull the tooth and be done with it! We have a 10 a.m. tee time at the best golf course in town, and it's 9:30 already…I don't have time to wait for the anesthetic to work!"

The dentist thinks to himself, "My goodness, this is surely a very brave man asking to have his tooth pulled without using anything to kill the pain" So the dentist asks him, "Which tooth is it, sir?"

The man turns to his wife and says, "Open your mouth, honey, and show him."

Sometimes we fail to comprehend the pain of those around us because of our own agenda.

August 9

There is one whose rash words are like sword thrusts, but the tongue of the wise brings healing (Proverbs 12:18, ESV).

Winston Churchill

One day when Winston Churchill was a young boy, he prepared for his father to inspect his collection of toy soldiers. He carefully arranged all the troops in the correct attack formations.

His father spent 20 minutes studying the scene. When he was finished, he asked Winston if he'd like to go into the Army, to which Winston enthusiastically said "yes."

For years Winston believed that his father had seen in him a talent for military genius. But he later found out that his father encouraged military college because he believed that Winston was not clever enough to pursue a career in law.

His father said that his son lacked the "cleverness, knowledge, and capacity for work. He has a talent for show-off, exaggeration, and make-believe."

The impression that you leave can have a lifetime effect…maybe affect the course of history. See the best in others, not the worst.

There are no limits to caring ®

August 10

Don't just pretend to love others. Really love them
(Romans 12:9, NLT).

Jack Benny

Jack Benny and his wife, Mary, were very close. On the morning after Jack Benny's death, Mary received a single long-stemmed rose from the local florist.

The very next morning, another rose was delivered to Mary, and again another was delivered the following morning. So, she called the florist to inquire about the roses.

The florist told her that before his death, her husband had made provision in his will that the florist would supply "one perfect red rose daily for the rest of Mary's life."

We are never promised tomorrow. Each day is a treasure, and we should never let a day pass without showing our loved ones how much we care.

Take time today to do something special for those special people in your life. Fold the laundry, make their favorite dish for supper, write an encouraging note, or buy a thoughtful gift.

August 11

Think about pure and lovely things and dwell on the fine, good things in others. Think about all you can praise God for and be glad about (Philippians 4:8, TLB).

Carnegie

Andrew Carnegie came to America from his homeland, Scotland, when he was a small boy. He worked hard and eventually became the largest steel manufacturer in the country. And he also became the wealthiest man in America at that time.

At one time he had 43 millionaires working for him. A reporter asked Carnegie how he had developed those 43 employees into valuable workers who all became millionaires themselves.

Carnegie replied that men are developed the same way gold is mined. When gold is mined, several tons of dirt must be removed in order to get to the gold. But one doesn't go into a mine looking for dirt - one goes in looking for the gold.

Likewise, look for the gold, not for the dirt…the good, not the bad. Don't look for the flaws and blemishes. The more good qualities we look for in others, the more gold we will discover in others.

There are no limits to caring ®

August 12

First, take the plank out of your own eye, and then you will see clearly to remove the speck from your brother's eye (Matthew 7:5, NIV).

The Window

Mary and her husband moved into a new neighborhood. The next morning at breakfast, Mary was looking out her window and saw her neighbor hanging her laundry outside to dry.

"That laundry is not very clean," Mary said to her husband. "She doesn't know how to wash correctly. Someone should teach her how to do laundry."

For the next several days, every time her neighbor hung her wash to dry, Mary would make the same comments, disapproving of her
neighbor's poor washing habits.

A few days later, Mary was surprised to see nice clean laundry on her neighbor's line, and she said to her husband, "Look! Our neighbor has finally learned how to wash correctly."

Her husband replied, "No, I got up early this morning and cleaned our windows!" Before giving criticism, check your view. If you are always seeing the bad in others, you may need to clean up *your* perspective.

August 13

No one pours new wine into old wineskins. Otherwise, the wine will burst the skins . . . No, they pour new wine into new wineskins (Mark 2:22, NIV).

Boll Weevil

In the mid-1920s, the boll weevil had made its way to the southern parts of Alabama and had all but destroyed most of the cotton crops

It was also during this time that people were feeling the effects of the Great Depression. The boll weevil just contributed to the economic woes of the Southern farmers at that time.

Farmers were spending time and money planting large cotton crops, only to have them destroyed by the boll weevils. People lost their livelihoods, their homes and were plunged into poverty.

But the boll weevil infestation did not entirely destroy Southern farmers. Because cotton crops were affected so badly, farmers began planting peanut crops, which flourished. Enterprise, Alabama even erected the Boll Weevil Monument because the boll weevils helped turn their economy around with the peanut crops.

We don't always understand why bad things happen. But it is often through difficult circumstances that new opportunities begin to grow.

August 14

Having gifts that differ according to the grace given to us, let us use them (Romans 12:6, ESV).

The Far Side

As a child, Gary Larson loved reading comic books and was very fond of keeping exotic pets such as snakes, frogs, and spiders. He loved animals so much that he began drawing them in his spare time.

After graduation from college, Gary wasn't sure what to do. He played in a band and worked in a music store for several years. This was not getting him anywhere.

So he took two days off to reflect on his career. On an impulse, he decided to submit his cartoons to *The Seattle Times*. He waited for them to call, convinced that his cartoons would fail. A few days later, the newspaper called...they loved the cartoons and would publish them weekly.

Larson sent his cartoon strip to another newspaper, where it was renamed "The Far Side" and went on to become a best-selling comic strip.

Don't let fear of failure stop you. Find your gift and reach for your goals.

August 15

This is love, not that we have loved God but that he loved us and sent his Son (1 John 4:10, ESV).

What is Love?

A group of children were asked the meaning of love. Here's what they said.

Rebecca - age 8 said, "When my grandmother got arthritis, she couldn't bend over and paint her toenails anymore. So my grandfather does it for her all the time, even when his hands got arthritis too."

Chrissy - age 6 said, "Love is when you go out to eat and give everybody most of your french fries without making them give you any of theirs."

Terri - age 4 said, "Love is what makes you smile when you're tired."

Bobby - age 7 said, "Love is what's in the room with you at Christmas if you stop opening presents and listen."

Mary - age 4 said, "Love is when your puppy licks your face even after you've left him alone all day."

Jessica - age 8 said, "You really shouldn't say 'I love you' unless you mean it. But if you mean it, you should say it a lot."

August 16

And when you pray, go into your room and shut the door and pray to your Father who is in secret. And your Father who sees in secret will reward you (Matthew 6:6, ESV).

Natalie Coughlin

Natalie Coughlin (pronounced Cog – lin) is a 12-time Olympic medalist. She won three golds, four silvers, and five bronze. In a recent interview, she was asked where she kept her medals. She went over to her chest of drawers, rummaged through her socks, and pulled out the medals.

Surprised, the interviewer asked why she did not display her medals for everyone to see. Natalie explained that she was indeed very proud of her medals. But she did not need to display them for all to see because everyone knew that she had won them. She did not need their praise because she knew her accomplishments.

Instead, she kept them in her drawer as a personal reminder of her achievements.

How do you handle your accomplishments? Do you display them for all to see because you need the praise of others? Or do your victories quietly motivate you for the next challenge?

August 17

Hardworking farmers should be the first to enjoy the fruit of their labor (2 Timothy 2:6, NLT).

Samuel Goldwyn

Sam was born August 17, 1879, in Warsaw and was the oldest of six children. At 15, his father died and soon after, Sam left home on foot and penniless. He traveled to England where he lived with relatives and worked long hours in a blacksmith shop to earn money to come to America.

At 19, Sam arrived in New York where he worked in a glove factory and, because of his hard work, he soon became a successful glove dealer.

Sam visited a nickelodeon and was so fascinated that he began thinking about a film career. So with hard work and determination, he pursued that dream.

Sam Goldwyn had an instrumental role in the formation of the two largest Hollywood studios: Paramount Pictures and Metro-Goldwyn-Mayer.

Sam Goldwyn said, "The harder I work, the luckier I get!"

August 18

I will instruct you and teach you in the way you should go
(Psalm 32:8, ESV).

Change Begins with a Choice

Ever feel like you are "locked-in"? Need a change in your life? Well, change is only a choice away. Think about it.

Any day we want we can choose to step outside of our comfort zone and experience new things. We can open our minds to learn more and to new possibilities, reach out and meet new people, and make new friends.

Or, we can choose not to. We can do nothing and remain as we are. The choice is ours.

Max DuPree, businessman and writer says, "We cannot become what we want to be by remaining what we are."

Want a change in your life today? You have the ability to choose what is best for yourself. God says, "I will teach you the way you should go; I will instruct you and advise you." You are not alone. God will give you the strength you need to begin today in making a positive change.

August 19

Consider it pure joy, my brothers and sisters, whenever you face trials of many kinds because you know that the testing of your faith produces perseverance (James 1:2-3, NIV).

David Longaberger

As a child, David struggled with a learning disability and a speech impairment. When he was in seventh grade, his class project was to sell magazine subscriptions for a school fund-raiser.

But David stuttered terribly, so he decided not to participate in the fund-raiser. But then he discovered that the person who sold the most subscriptions would win a radio. David wanted that radio very badly, so he became determined to win the prize, overcoming his fear of ridicule and rejection.

David went door to door selling subscriptions all over town. The more excited he became, the more he stuttered, and the harder he tried to convince people to purchase the subscriptions.

David sold the most subscriptions and won the radio. Today he is known as David Longaberger, the owner of the basket manufacturing firm the Longaberger Company.

David later said that his perseverance and confidence came from realizing that success is about overcoming the things that hinder you.

August 20

The end of the matter; all has been heard. Fear God and keep his commandments, for this is the whole duty of man (Ecclesiastes 12:13, ESV).

Searching

Solomon was the son of David. Both were Kings of Israel. Solomon was known for his great wisdom. He was into economic development and was very successful. He built cities, the Temple in Jerusalem, and much more. In addition, he had 1,000 wives and concubines.

A thousand wives would cause some of us to question his wisdom. Nevertheless, Solomon had it all; he had success, wealth, power, and sexual satisfaction. But he was searching for meaning and purpose in this own life.

He wrote the book of Ecclesiastes and, in essence, asked the question, "What's it all about?" He had it all, but he was still searching.

Do you find yourself searching for value and meaning in life? You may have it all and come up empty. Solomon found that it was his relationship with God that brought him peace and meaning in his life.

Stuff fades away, but our faith in God makes everything meaningful.

August 21

Be angry and do not sin (Ephesians 4:26, ESV).

Anger

She was just an ordinary 14-year-old. But on this day, she was having problems with her dad. She became angry and went into her room and slammed the door so hard that it came back and made a hole in the wall. Now she didn't mean to slam the doorknob through the wall; she was just angry.

She was soon over her anger and all was well between her and her dad.

But every time she closed her bedroom door, she would see the small hole that the doorknob had made in the wall.

That's what anger does when it is not handled well.

How do you handle your anger? Does it leave permanent scars on the people you live with or work with?

The Bible says, "Be angry and sin not." Anger is an emotion, not a sin. But the way we handle our anger can be damaging to those about us.

August 22

Lazy people don't even cook the game they catch, but the diligent make use of everything they find (Proverbs 12:27, NLT).

College Dreams

Allyson put her dreams of attending college on hold when she got married and had 11 children. Now, at 50 years old, she completed one degree and is now attending Harvard. In addition, she commutes 4,000 miles each week from her home in Oklahoma to Harvard in Massachusetts.

Allyson credits three things for her success. She wakes early each day to read the Bible, go for a run, and then seize the day. She says she won't let anyone steal her mojo for the day.

She keeps a positive and determined attitude, and she praises her supportive network of family and friends. And Allyson refuses to short-change her kids. She makes their breakfast each morning and won't crack a textbook until they have gone to sleep.

It's never too late to pursue your goals. Work hard, be determined. Don't let anything hold you back.

August 23

Two are better than one because they have a good return for their labor (Ecclesiastes 4:9, NIV).

Team

A man got lost while driving in the country. While trying to read his map, he ran off the road into a ditch and got stuck. He walked to a nearby farm for help.

The farmer said, "Sure, old Clem can get you out of that ditch," pointing to his old mule. So, the man, the farmer, and the mule made their way to the stuck car. The farmer hitched the mule to the car. He snapped the reins and shouted, "Pull Fred, Pull Jack, Pull Ted, Pull Clem!" and the old mule easily pulled the car from the ditch.

The man was thankful but amazed, "Why did you call all those other names before you called Clem?" The Farmer grinned and said, "Old Clem is just about blind. So as long as he believes he's part of a team, he doesn't mind pulling."

What could we pull if we really pulled together?

There are no limits to caring ®

August 24

Our bodies have many parts, and God has put each part just where he wants it. How strange a body would be if it had only one part! (1 Corinthians 12:18-19, NLT).

John Mark Stallings

At the dedication of one of our group homes, our distinguished guests were Coach Gene Stallings, head football coach at the University of Alabama, and his son John Mark.

Several years ago, John Mark passed away. He was a person with an intellectual disability! But his disability never stopped him. His dad didn't leave him at home but made him a part of a normal family life.

In 1992, when Alabama won a national championship, John Mark was on the sidelines, on national television, with his dad. What a beautiful picture!

The coach and father embraced his son and enabled him to live his life to the fullest.

As they drove to the group home dedication in Greenville, John Mark glanced at his dad and said, "Just you and me Pop. Just you and me." Coach Stallings and John Mark taught us more than how to win a national championship. They taught us how to win in life.

August 25

Be strong and courageous and do the work. Do not be afraid or discouraged, for the LORD God . . . is with you
(1 Chronicles 28:20, ESV).

Courageous Friend

Nicole and Dale were swimming at the beach with their church group one afternoon.

Twelve-year-old Nicole was floating on her boogie board when she heard her friend, Dale, calling for help. He had been caught in a rip current and was weak from fighting the water.

So, Nicole swam to Dale and helped him onto the board. Together, they struggled to swim back to shore. But suddenly, a wave slammed into them, knocking them off the board. Nicole pulled herself back up, but Dale disappeared into the water.

Nicole made it to shore, but it took rescuers several minutes to find Dale and later get him to a hospital. He made a full recovery.

A true friend helps you brave the turbulent waters. Maybe you know someone who needs your friendship. Be a courageous friend right now.

There are no limits to caring ®

August 26

Do your best to present yourself to God as one approved, a worker who has no need to be ashamed (2 Timothy 2:15, ESV).

Cathy Rigby

Cathy Rigby was a member of the U.S. Women's Gymnastics Team in the 1972 Olympics at Munich. She had trained very hard for several years and was determined to win a gold medal.

She was determined not to let herself or her country down. She performed well, but when it was all over and the winners were announced, her name was not among them. Cathy was crushed.

Afterward, she joined her parents in the stands, discouraged and despairing over her defeat. As she sat down, she told her parents, "I'm sorry. I did my best."

Her mother looked her straight in the eyes and said ten words that Cathy says she will never forget: "Doing your best is more important than being the best."

Words of affirmation from a parent make all the difference. Having parents who know how to affirm a child is a huge blessing. Some have never had that affirming experience.

August 27

It is God who works in you to will and to act in order to fulfill his good purpose (Philippians 2:13, NIV).

Cake Mix

A little boy came in from school and started telling his Grandma about his terrible day. He had nothing but problems – all day long.

Grandma was baking a cake. She asked the boy if he would like a snack. "Here, have some cooking oil." "Yuck, Grandma!" "Well, then have some raw eggs." "That's gross!" "Would you like some flour or some baking soda?" "Grandma, those are yucky!"

Then Grandmother replied, "Yes, by themselves, those things seem yucky. But when they are put together in the right way, they turn into a delicious cake! That's the way life is."

Separately, many events in our lives seem difficult or even wrong. But together, with the right mix, they turn into something else altogether. Look over your life and notice how some events, which were not pleasant, led to other events that were good.

August 28

Do not be anxious about anything (Philippians 4:6, NIV).

Meat Cutter Stress

One day a meat cutter was working to catch up on special orders. In his haste, he accidentally backed into his meat cutting machine. His response was, "I think I just got a little behind in my work!"

Getting a little behind in our work can be painful. It can be overwhelming. Life can be stressful when you are under pressure. What do we do with our stress? We can dump it on our families or our co-workers. That will certainly create more stress. Or, we can take responsibility for our stress and determine healthy ways to deal with it.

It could mean beginning an exercise program. Maybe do more reading. Whatever it means, it is important that I do not dump my stress on other people, no matter how much behind I get in my work!

August 29

Jesus replied, "What is impossible with man is possible with God" (Luke 18:27, NIV).

Possible

An elementary teacher asked her students what they wanted to be when they grew up. The usual responses came from all over the room.

"A football player." "A doctor." "A teacher." "An Astronaut." "The president." "A fireman."

Everyone had a response except little Tommy, who was sitting quietly and still. So she asked, "Tommy, what do you want to be when you grow up?" "Possible," Tommy replied. "Possible?" asked the teacher. "Yes," Tommy said. "My mom is always telling me I'm 'impossible.' So when I get to be big, I want to be possible."

There are times when children do seem to be "impossible." However, they don't need to hear that word from a parent or any other adult in their lives. We need to do all we can to enable children to see unlimited possibilities. Today give a positive word of encouragement. Help a child feel possible! Perhaps we should see no one as impossible.

August 30

By insolence comes nothing but strife, but with those who take advice is wisdom (Proverbs 13:10, ESV).

Bill Gates Says

Bill Gates, who is one of the world's richest men, said some things about life directed toward the younger generation.

1. Life is not fair; get used to it.

2. If you think your teacher is tough, wait 'till you get a boss. He doesn't have tenure.

3. Flipping burgers is not beneath your dignity. Your grandparents had a different word for burger flipping; they called it opportunity.

4. Life is not divided into semesters. You don't get summers off, and very few employers are interested in helping you find yourself. You'll have to do that on your own time.

5. Television is not real life. In real life, people actually have to leave the coffee shop and go to jobs.

6. Be nice to nerds. Chances are you'll end up working for one!

Bill Gates didn't say it, but it's also true there are no limits to caring.

August 31

Watch yourselves closely so that you do not forget the things your eyes have seen or let them fade from your heart as long as you live. Teach them to your children and to their children (Deuteronomy 4:9, NIV).

Don't Throw the Baby Out with the Bath Water

Only in modern times have people taken a bath frequently. Many folks would wait until the weather warmed up in late spring or summer before taking a bath.

A big tub was filled with hot water. The men of the house had the privilege of the clean water, then the women, and then the children. Last of all, the babies. By then, the water was so dirty you could actually lose a baby in it. Hence the saying, "don't throw the baby out with the bathwater."

Today our bathwater is dirty. We may have lost sight of our children. We may not be just throwing away our babies with the dirty water but also their future--public education. As a community, we need to make decisions that ensure that we are not throwing away our children and their future with dirty water.

Know what you are throwing away.

September 1

Come to me, all you who are weary and burdened, and I will give you rest (Matthew 11:28, NIV).

Labor Day

Labor Day weekend is almost here. A time when some of us will have a day off from work, in honor of "the working man." It is a time to celebrate the opportunity that we have to be able to work. Our work provides for our families and builds this great nation.

We all need to rest, to rejuvenate. A time for re-creation. God created for six days and rested on the seventh. Just look at a plant or a tree…it's always being recreated. So should we be re-created…rejuvenated?

Each of us needs a time of rest. What do you do to rest, re-create or rejuvenate yourself? Find a way…you'll like what it does for you.

Jesus said, "Come unto me all of you who are weary and burdened, and I will give you rest." Why not take him up on that invitation?

September 2

When they were discouraged, I smiled at them. My look of approval was precious to them (Job 29:24, NLT).

Makeover

Have you seen the makeover TV shows where people undergo surgery, liposuction, and other things to look physically beautiful?

Well, it's not just for people anymore. Now some farmers are resorting to plastic surgery to beautify their cattle so they can win the grand prize in cattle shows. The Tasmania Agricultural Show had to enforce rules against it. They believe that animals should have "natural attractiveness."

Our world is obsessed with beauty. And it can make us feel so inadequate.

Someone once said, "Of all the things you wear, your expression is the most important."

Just think, today, your smile could be the brightest part of someone's life. You might not be able to afford the latest in designer wear or make a glamorous fashion statement. But how much does it cost to smile? That's really the best of all fashion statements. That's when you look your best. Smile today, and the world will smile with you.

September 3

Let the words of my mouth and the meditation of my heart be acceptable in your sight (Psalm 19:14, ESV).

Body Piercing

Students in a third-grade class were asking their teacher about her newly pierced ears.

"Does the hole go all the way through?" "Yes," the teacher replied.
"Did it hurt?" "Just a little," the teacher said. "Did they stick a needle through your ears?" "No, they used a special gun." Oooh, "How far away did they stand?"

We have to be careful with what we say to children. They tend to hear things more literally than adults. Of course, it doesn't hurt to monitor what we say to adults as well. No one wants to be misunderstood. Good communication requires practice.

Practice good communication today by clearly telling how much you appreciate a loved one or friend. It is hard to misunderstand words like "I love you," "I care about you," or "Thank you." Practice good communication.

September 4

If we say we have fellowship with him while we walk in darkness, we lie and do not practice truth (1 John 1:6, ESV).

Albert Schweitzer

Reporters and city officials gathered at a Chicago railroad station to meet the 1952 Nobel Peace Prize winner. When the train arrived, a man with bushy hair and a large mustache stepped from the train. Cameras flashed.

The man politely thanked them and then, looking over their heads, excused himself. He quickly walked through the crowd to an elderly black woman who was struggling with two large suitcases. He picked up the bags and escorted the woman to a bus, helping her aboard.

The man was Dr. Albert Schweitzer, the famous missionary doctor who had spent his life helping the poor in Africa. In response to Schweitzer's action, one member of the reception committee said with great admiration, "That's the first time I ever saw a sermon walking."

Talk is cheap. Being a servant isn't. Serving others is not the most popular idea in today's society. Be a servant and demonstrate there are no limits to caring.

September 5

Make the most of every opportunity (Ephesians 5:16, NLT).

Woody Woodpecker

A man and his wife were on their honeymoon. Each night when the couple went to bed, a woodpecker would begin pecking away at the trees around their cabin. The man wanted to shoot the bird. His wife suggested he make a cartoon about the bird instead.

On that day, Woody Woodpecker was created. One of the most adored cartoons of past generations.

How do we look at each situation that we are presented with? Do we throw the towel in and let anger or frustration get the best of us? Do we simply give up instead of pressing through a little while longer?

Think of all the wonderful things that could happen when we choose to embrace situations we're faced with… with optimism… to learn from and get the most out of these moments.

Surround yourself with people who will encourage you to find and make the best out of everything in your life.

September 6

Sing praises to God, sing praises! Sing praises to our King, sing praises! (Psalm 47:6, ESV).

Doxology

In the 17th Century, London suffered two great disasters. In 1665, there was an outbreak of the Bubonic Plague, which spread from parish to parish and killed thousands of people. The Bubonic Plague was known as the Black Death, and it was a terrible way to die. In all, 15% of the population in the summer of 1665 died.

The next year was worse. A fire started on September 1, 1666. The summer had been hot and dry, and the environment was ripe for a great fire. When the fire was brought under control on September 6, 80% of London had been destroyed. Hundreds of thousands of people were left homeless.

Then in 1674, eight years later, Thomas Ken wrote the great hymn called "Doxology."

Praise God, from Whom all blessings flow;
Praise Him, all creatures here below;
Praise Him above, ye heavenly host;
Praise Father, Son, and Holy Ghost.

When our world is destroyed, we will find peace when we praise God...regardless of the circumstances.

September 7

Whoever spares the rod hates their children, but the one who loves their children is careful to discipline them (Proverbs 13:24, NIV).

Giraffe

When a giraffe is born, it falls 10 feet from its mother's womb and usually lands on its back.

The mother giraffe then positions herself directly over her calf and then kicks her baby so that it is sent tumbling head over heels.

The process is repeated over and over again as the baby struggles to rise. Finally, the calf stands for the first time on its wobbly legs.

Then the mother giraffe does the unthinkable. She kicks her baby off its feet again. Why? She wants it to remember how to get up quickly so that it can stay with the herd.

This parenting may seem cruel, but love says that it's the only way to ensure the future survival of that giraffe.

We must love our children enough to let them fall so they can learn to get up. This may be the only way to learn. Simply to rescue is not always the best way to love.

September 8

Let the greatest among you become as the youngest and the leader as one who serves (Luke 22:26, ESV).

Leadership

There is a dire shortage of leadership. Leadership is the art of removing barriers and empowering people. So much can be achieved when leaders actually lead.

What if great leaders over the centuries had refused to lead?

Unfortunately, leadership is too often about waiting until there's a crisis and seeing who can be blamed. Leadership is not about taking a popularity poll to discover what ought to be done. Leadership is about leading where we must go, even when the going is not popular but right.

We will never solve the crisis in education, the crisis in mental health, the injustice caused by an antiquated tax system or a flawed state constitution without visionary leadership.

Leadership doesn't wait for the masses to say what has to be done; leadership guides the masses to resolving the issues. Visionary leadership understands that there are no limits to caring – for people.

September 9

The man asked him, "What is your name?" (Genesis 32:27, NIV).

Who Am I

A college student took a course on bird watching because he heard that it was an easy class. Unfortunately, on his first day, he learned that there was a new professor. This new professor was very demanding and required them to purchase four very expensive textbooks.

The next day the students were required to read the first four chapters in each book. The professor then gave a pop quiz.

On the quiz, there were pictures of only the bird's legs, without their bodies. The students had to identify each bird based on its legs.

The student was frustrated and jumped up to leave. The professor stopped him, asking him to return to his seat.

The student explained that he just couldn't handle the class anymore.

The professor asked, "What is your name?" The student pulled up his pants leg and said, "You tell me."

Who am I? It has everything to do with the way we walk, not the way we talk.

September 10

Whatever you do, do it all for the glory of God (1 Corinthians 10:31, NIV).

Bagpipes

Robert played the bagpipes and was asked to play at a funeral for a homeless man who had no family or friends.

Robert got lost on the way to the cemetery and finally arrived an hour late. The funeral director had gone, and only the gravediggers and crew were there.

Robert went to the side of the grave and looked down. The vault lid was already in place. So he started to play. The workers gathered around as Robert played "Amazing Grace," like never before, for this homeless man.

The workers began to weep, and Robert cried with them. Robert finished and headed for his car. As he was leaving, he heard one of the workers say, "I never seen nothin' like that before. For over 20 years I've been putting in septic tanks."

In everything you do, give your all because you never know who you will impact.

September 11

When the righteous cry for help, the LORD hears and delivers them out of all their troubles (Psalm 34:17, ESV).

Call for Help

Jack and Shane were leaving football practice at Missouri Western when they saw a woman across the street frantically beating on her car window with a bat.

They decided to turn around and see if the woman needed any help. When they stopped, the woman told them she had accidentally locked her 17-month-old grandson in the car. The toddler was sick from the heat and beginning to lose consciousness.

Shane quickly grabbed the bat from the woman and, with one swing, broke the window and pulled out her grandson, who has now made a full recovery.

The woman, Teresa, thanked the boys, saying that she had been trying to break the window and desperately prayed that God would send her some help.

Every day there are people all around us who are desperate for help. God is calling, will you answer?

September 12

Do not be overcome by evil, but overcome evil with good
(Romans 12:21, ESV).

Jesse Owens

In 1936, Jesse Owens competed in the Olympics in the face of racial discrimination.

Jesse was born September 12, 1913, in Alabama. He began running in high school and joined the track team. As a senior in high school, Jesse tied the world record in the 100-yard dash. At a track meet in 1935, he set three world records. He had accomplished what had never been done before.

Jesse Owens entered the 1936 Olympics, which were held in Nazi Germany. Hitler was going to prove to the world that the German people were the dominant race. Jesse had different plans, and that year, he became the first American in the history of Olympic Track and Field to win four gold medals.

Jesse Owens was the son of a sharecropper and grandson of a slave. He overcame circumstances and won the gold. He showed that we cannot let circumstances defeat us.

September 13

God teaches people through suffering and uses distress to open their eyes (Job 36:15, GNT).

Tony Dungy

When Tony Dungy was coach of the Indiana Colts, he gave a speech at a breakfast ceremony on the morning before the Super Bowl.

He spoke about lessons he'd learned from his youngest son, Jordan, who has a rare condition that causes him to feel no pain. Dungy said, "We've learned a lot about pain since we've had Jordan.

For example, Jordan loves cookies, and they are good. So he will go right to the oven, reach in, take the pan out, burn his hands and eat the cookies and burn his tongue and never feel it. He doesn't know what will hurt him.

The coach said, "We've learned some hurts are necessary for kids to find out the difference between what's good and what's harmful."

People wonder why God allows pain in our lives, why bad things happen to good people. The lesson is simple. In pain, we learn what's good and what's not.

September 14

Be not among drunkards or among gluttonous eaters of meat (Proverbs 23:20, ESV).

Obesity

What are some of the major diseases that we have seen in our country? The Spanish Influenza in 1918 killed over 500,000 people. Polio spread like an epidemic in the 1950s, killing thousands and leaving many survivors to face lifelong complications.

Today we have heart disease, stroke, hypertension, diabetes. The interesting thing is that most of these diseases can be prevented.

The number one health issue today is obesity, and it is rising across the county, more so in Mississippi and Alabama than any other state. And obesity often leads to these diseases that can take your life.

The more you eat, the shorter your life span. In a real sense, we are a county that is eating ourselves to death. Each one of us has a responsibility to eat healthily and to teach our children good eating habits. Change the way you eat today and be on the way to a happier, healthier, and longer life.

September 15

The leech has two suckers that cry out, "More, more!"
(Proverbs 30:15, NLT).

Fireproof

In the movie *Fireproof*, Caleb and Catherine's marriage is headed for divorce. In a final effort to save his marriage, Caleb begins a 40-day study called *Love Dare*. One of the lessons read:

> *"Watch out for parasites. A parasite is anything that latches onto you or your partner and sucks the life out of your marriage. They're normally in the form of addictions like gambling, drugs, or pornography. They promise pleasure but grow like a disease and consume more and more of your thoughts, time, and money. They steal away your loyalty and your heart from those you love. Marriages rarely survive if parasites are present."*

Do you have a parasite sucking the life out of your marriage?
- An addiction
- Gambling
- Alcohol or Drugs
- A lover
- Fantasies
- A friend
- Work
- Pleasures

Parasites steal your heart from your spouse. Marriages can't survive a parasite. Whatever that parasite may be, destroy it now or it will destroy your relationship.

September 16

Cast your burden on the LORD, and he will sustain you
(Psalm 55:22, ESV).

Burdens

A professor raised a glass of water and asked, "How heavy is this glass of water?"

The answers varied and he replied, "The weight doesn't matter; it depends on how long you hold it. If I hold it for a minute, it's not a problem; after an hour, my arm may begin to ache; after a day, I may need medical attention. The glass weighs the same, but the longer I hold it, the heavier it becomes."

So it is with burdens and stresses in our lives. The longer we hold onto them, the more difficult they become until finally, we are unable to carry on. We all have issues in our lives that we wish were not there. The world we live in causes a great amount of stress, and we bring stress on ourselves.

We can't simply ignore it. Get organized, don't pass it around to others, prioritize your life. Take care of yourself with daily exercise and a balanced diet.

September 17

[A time for every matter under heaven] a time to embrace, and a time to refrain from embracing (Ecclesiastes 3:5, ESV).

Hug

Xavier was hosting a party with several friends at his home. They were sitting on the patio, enjoying steak, shrimp, and fine wine when suddenly a hooded man came through the back gate, pointed a gun at them, and demanded money.

Without hesitating, one of the guests blurted out, "Why don't you have a glass of wine with us?" So, the intruder took a glass of wine and sipped it, then helped himself to some food. After a few minutes, he tucked his gun away and suddenly asked for a hug.

Each of the stunned guests stood up and wrapped their arms around him. Before leaving, the intruder complemented the food and wine one last time and then asked for a group hug. The five guests all surrounded him with hugs.

With that, he walked out with his glass of wine, leaving the bewildered guests unharmed and very confused. Hugs can be powerful. They can stop violence, demonstrate compassion, and bring people together.

September 18

He will renew your life and sustain you in your old age
(Ruth 4:15, NIV).

Age

Years ago, I visited my grandmother in a nursing home. She was 92 at the time. I said, "Grandma, are there any old people here?" She thought a minute, "Yes, there is one who is 98 and one who is 96." For some reason, she didn't see herself in that number.

To her, age is something in your mind. As Mark Twain said, "Age is an issue of mind over matter. If you don't mind, it doesn't matter."

How old would you be if you didn't know how old you are?

C.S. Lewis said, "You are never too old to set another goal or to dream a new dream." Do you have a new dream? A new goal? Live it!!

As Abraham Lincoln, who by the way died at the age of 56, once said, "It's not the years in your life that count. It's the life in your years."

How much life and energy do you have for this day?

September 19

God is our refuge and strength, a very present help in trouble. Therefore we will not fear (Psalm 46:1-2, ESV).

Bethany Hamilton

Bethany Hamilton was a 13-year-old girl who loved to surf. But one day, while surfing, she was attacked by a shark and lost her arm…almost her life.

But less than a month later she, was back in the water. She was not going to let her fear keep her away from her love of surfing. But it was a challenge to learn how to rebalance her body on the surfboard.

Bethany was optimistic and she worked diligently, overcoming her fear of the water. She credits her faith in God for her success.

But she didn't stop there. She used her story to inspire many to overcome their own fears. She wanted to be a good role model demonstrating courage over fear and hope over hopelessness.

Bethany now views her misfortune as a blessing.

Only God can take our tragedies and turn them into something really good.

September 20

I press on toward the goal (Philippians 3:14, ESV).

Kobayashi

It was 12 o clock noon on a hot July day, and a major sporting event was about to take place…a hotdog eating contest.

Takeru Kobayashi, a small Japanese man weighing only 112 pounds, was set to compete against the biggest and best eaters in the world. It was doubtful that he would win.

The competition began, and Kobayashi rapidly scarfed down hotdog after hotdog with steely determination. Amazingly he won, by eating over 50 hotdogs in just 12 minutes. It was a new record. He gained 17 pounds in the process.

After the contest, the hotdog stuffed Kobayashi was asked what he planned to do next. His reply? "Ice cream!"

Setting goals that seem too far out of reach may be the best way to realize your potential. But when you do achieve your goal, don't stop there. Something even sweeter may lie ahead. Be all you can be.

September 21

Therefore encourage one another (1 Thessalonians 4:18, ESV).

Worth It

When I spoke at a church recently, a person with a disability came by and said to me, "You said 'I was worth it' but I didn't think I was worth it. Am I really worth it?" I said, "Yes, you are worth it."

When people have a disability or other characteristic that causes them to look different and be seen as different, they may have a low opinion of themselves. And there are times when all of us feel somewhat worthless.

But each of us, regardless of our circumstances, has value and worth. God created us that way.

It is important that we respond to each other as having value and worth. It is important that we help build up each other's self-esteem. Say something uplifting to those about you…because they are worth it…and so are you.

Make it a great day by showing others they are worth it.

September 22

Unless you turn and become like children, you will never enter the kingdom of heaven (Matthew 18:3, ESV).

Kindergarten lessons

Robert Fulghum, author of the book *All I Really Need to Know I Learned in Kindergarten*, wrote that most of what he needed to know about life he learned in kindergarten. Wisdom is not achieved in graduate school but in the sandbox at nursery school.

He went on to describe the lessons he learned in kindergarten: Share everything, Play fair, Don't hit people, Put things back where you found them, Clean up your own mess, Don't take things that aren't yours, Say you're sorry when you hurt somebody . . . When you go out into the world, watch for traffic, hold hands, and stick together.

That's what the man meant over two thousand years ago when he said, "…unless you become like little children…"

Those simple lessons learned as children are some of the most important lessons one will ever learn. The best lessons are the simple ones.

September 23

Finally, all of you have unity of mind, sympathy, brotherly love, a tender heart, and a humble mind (1 Peter 3:8, ESV).

Valdez

After the Exxon Valdez oil spill in Alaska, the communities around Prince William Sound experienced many changes. Depression increased, substance abuse became epidemic, crime rose, and family ties and friendships were destroyed.

Years later, the damage remains. However, healing is happening. How? By creating what Dr. Steven Picou of the University of South Alabama calls a Therapeutic Community, a community of trust and support.

Together we have weathered many natural disasters, and the experiences have made us stronger, closer, and more caring.

There is a strange thing about technological disasters; they tend to have the opposite effect. They pull us apart. But we can choose not to let that happen. We can choose to work together, help one another, and not let a disaster destroy our greatest treasure; our community.

September 24

Choose life that you and your offspring may live
(Deuteronomy 30:19, ESV).

Blind Determination

Mr. Wilson spends hours in his garden every day. That is his passion, to grow his own food. And his garden is quite large, spanning over an acre.

But Mr. Wilson is 77 years old and he is blind too. Each morning he rises before dawn and crawls on his hands and knees to tend to his garden. He has learned to feel the difference between peas, beans, and tomatoes.

He says it is a way of life for him. And with the current economy, he hopes younger generations will learn the importance and the pride in growing their own food.

He says that if a blind 77-year-old man can do it, then there are plenty of others who can find the time to do it too.

That's what you call determination. Life is really a matter of perspective...how you see it. You can be a victim or victorious ...your choice.

September 25

Your abundance at the present time should supply their need so that their abundance may supply your need, that there may be fairness (2 Corinthians 8:15, ESV).

Fairness

When I was five, my sister and I were playing outdoors at my great aunt's house. I found a cigarette pack stuffed with coins. I was elated and took the coins to my aunt. She counted out the money and divided it between my sister and me. When it didn't divide evenly, she made up the difference from her own pocket.

This provided me a lesson about fairness, ethics, and giving. My aunt was poor. She could have kept the coins; legally they were hers. I could have kept the coins and not told or shared. Ethically, they were mine. I found them. But my aunt knew something about the joy of giving, and she shared.

Her example brought the concepts of fairness, ethics, and giving all together, fleshed them out in a way I could never forget. We need more people like her. We need to demonstrate an ethical and charitable lifestyle.

September 26

Learn to do right; seek justice. Defend the oppressed. Take up the cause of the fatherless; plead the case of the widow (Isaiah 1:17, NIV).

Circle of Friends

A few years ago, in Africa, a 12-year-old girl had been missing for nearly a week. Police and relatives searched for her. They all feared the worst.

When she was found on the outskirts of the town, the rescue team had discovered something remarkably strange. Lions were standing guard over her. As the rescuers began to approach, the lions simply left her-- like a gift --and went back into the forest!

She had been taken and beaten repeatedly by seven men. If the lions had not come to her rescue, then it could have been much worse.

Just as the lions watched over the little girl, it is our responsibility to look out for those in need.

- Those who have been beaten down by life.
- Those who find themselves in a hopeless situation.

Those need a circle of strong friends—like you can be.

September 27

The years of our life are seventy, or even by reason of strength eighty (Psalm 90:10, ESV).

Aging

How old are you? How old would you be if you didn't know how old you are?

When we are young, we think we have a lifetime to live… a long time. But when we get old, we ask the question, "How did I get old so quickly?" Life is short.

The psalmist said our days are "three score and ten" …seventy years. But if God gives you a bonus… fifth quarter, what will you do with it? Live for self or live for God?

The way we serve God when we are old is just as important as when we are young. We need a great start, but we also need to finish well. How we finish determines the score.

Jesus taught that when you serve the least of these, you serve him.

Serve one another…the least of these… when you are young and old!

It is not over til it's over. Finish well.

September 28

Therein are some things hard to understand (2 Peter 3:16, KJV).

Explanations

Attending a wedding for the first time, a little girl whispered to her mother, "Why is the bride dressed in white?" "Because white is a color of happiness, and today is the happiest day of her life," the mother tried to explain, keeping it simple.

The child thought about this for a minute, then said, "So why is the groom wearing black?"

Some things are hard to explain. Not only do they not add up in a child's mind, but all of us also have difficulty making sense of some things in life.

The good news is that we do not have to have an explanation for everything. Most of us would be hard-pressed to give a scientific explanation for the formation of a rainbow, but that doesn't keep us from enjoying its beauty!

September 29

Love bears all things, believes all things, hopes all things, endures all things. Love never ends (1 Corinthians:13:7-8, ESV).

Love Defined

A friend recently asked a large number of her friends to define love.

Walt said, "Love is just a little thing; it's like a little lizard. It winds around your heart and nibbles on your gizzard."

Another, obviously a senior citizen from up north, said, "Love is having the toilet seat in the outhouse warmed when the snow is knee-deep, and the temperature is below zero."

Just what is love? We speak of loving our pets, loving popcorn, loving cool weather, loving our parents, loving our children. We make that little four-letter word cover a lot of ground!

A local of kindergarten children had some mature-sounding answers when asked to define love:

Brandon said, "Love is sharing things." Jacob said, "…doing the right thing." Nicky offered, "Love is to be good to people."

Those kids seem to know that love involves caring, and importantly, demonstrating that you care.

September 30

I have fought the good fight, I have finished the race, I have kept the faith (2 Timothy 4:7, ESV).

Needing Money

Mary came home one weekend from college to visit and left her biology book at home when she returned to school. Mary's father called her to tell her that he'd mail the book and some money.

"You don't have to mail the book," said Mary, "because I probably won't finish reading it." But Mary's dad encouraged her to finish her textbook. When he got off the phone, he wrote two checks and placed them in the book in a package, and then went to the post office.

When he returned home, Mary's mother asked, "How much did you give Mary?" Mary's dad replied, "I wrote two checks, one for $50, and the other for $1,000."

"But don't worry…I taped the $50 check to the cover of Mary's book. But I put the $1,000 somewhere between the pages in chapter 15…so she definitely won't find that one."

Stay committed. Finish what you start. Then you will surely reap the surprising benefits.

October 1

So they came and apologized to them (Acts 16:39, ESV).

I'm Sorry

"I'm sorry." Those were the words spoken by a father to a child. A wrong had occurred. "I'm sorry." Those were the words spoken by a husband to a wife. A wrong had occurred. "I'm sorry." Those were the words of an employee to a boss. A mistake had been made.

"I'm sorry" are words that indicate responsibility, humility, and maturity. We all make mistakes, and to be able to take responsibility ensures a healthy relationship.

Not every person is big enough to say, "I'm sorry." Those words tell a great deal about the size of a person's heart and soul. Our ability, or inability, to apologize is a measure of how much we have grown as a human being.

When you find yourself at fault, don't forget to say, "I'm sorry." It will strengthen your relationship with others and make you feel better about yourself.

October 2

Live a life filled with love, following the example of Christ. He loved us and offered himself as a sacrifice for us, a pleasing aroma to God (Ephesians 5:2, NLT).

Porcupine

John Ortberg, *Everybody's Normal till You Get to Know Them* has an interesting perspective on the porcupine. The porcupine has around 30,000 quills attached to his body. Each quill can be driven into an enemy, the wounds can fester and be fatal.

The porcupine is not generally regarded as a lovable animal. Porcupines have two methods for handling relationships: Run or fight! They either head for a tree or stick out their quills. They are solitary animals.

But porcupines don't always want to be alone. In the late autumn, a young porcupine's thoughts turn to love. But love turns out to be a risky business when you're a porcupine.

This is the porcupine's dilemma: How do you get close without getting hurt? This is our dilemma, too. How do we love without being hurt? If you love, you will experience pain…The greater the love, the greater the grief. But love is worth it.

October 3

The Lord God said, "it is not good for the man to be alone" (Genesis 2:28, NIV).

Isolation

In Brazil lives a man who has been named "The most isolated man on the planet." He was discovered in 1996 by loggers working in that area. Government groups made contact, but their efforts resulted in confusion and violence.

Little is known about this man other than the fact that he is the last survivor of an uncontacted tribe of Indians. Unable to bridge the communication gap, the Brazilian government cordoned off the 31 square mile area surrounding him. It is his "safe zone." This land is not to be trespassed upon nor encroached upon by land developers.

There he remains alone and isolated.

Some of us choose to be isolated, alone. Even when it is in our best interest not to be alone. Some are isolated physically or even emotionally.

Don't let yourself become isolated. The tragedies and joys of life are better with the love and support that is found when we reach out to one another.

October 4

The house was filled with people weeping and wailing, but he said, "Stop the weeping! She isn't dead; she's only asleep (Luke 8:52, NLT).

Saved by the Bell

England was running out of places to bury people. So, they dug up coffins, removed the bones to a house, and reused the grave. In reopening these coffins, they discovered many had scratch marks on the inside and they realized they had been burying people alive.

So, they started tying a string on the corpses, ran it through the coffin up to the surface, and tied it to a bell. Someone would sit out in the graveyard all night to listen for the bell. Hence, we have the "graveyard shift" where someone was "saved by the bell," or he was a "dead ringer."

We would never bury anyone alive—or would we? Some people we treat as though they are dead—but they are alive with potential. If we listen, we can hear them ringing. Some have written off a generation of youth, but if you listen, you can hear potential. Listen for the bells.

October 5

I can do all things through him who strengthens me
(Philippians 4:13, ESV).

Madeline Albright

She was a poor refugee with little hope of being anything more. The possibility of her living very long and making any kind of significant contributions to the world was limited. After all, being a woman, she faced significant barriers, and being a poor refugee only complicated matters.

October 5, 2000, the Secretary of State, Madeline Albright, looked on with pride as Milosevic's government collapsed. She had significantly participated in removing Yugoslavian dictator Milosevic and presiding over the return of democracy to the very region her family once fled.

Much of what happened in Yugoslavia was Albright's victory, even though she gave credit to the people of Yugoslavia.

It doesn't really matter where you're from, which gender you are, how wealthy or poor you are, or who your parents may be; you can make a difference in your world right here, right now.

October 6

A party gives laughter, wine gives happiness, and money gives everything! (Ecclesiastes 10:19, NLT).

Help

Listen to some actual 911 calls:

One person called saying, "I made a ham and cheese sandwich and left it on the kitchen table. When I came back from the restroom, someone had taken a bite out of it. This has happened to me before, and I'm sick and tired of it!"

Another caller complained, "I'm trying to reach nine eleven, but my phone doesn't have an eleven on it." The dispatcher replied, "Nine eleven and nine-one-one are the same thing." The caller replied, "I may be old, but I'm not stupid."

One man called saying, "I'm having trouble breathing...I'm going to pass out." "An ambulance is on the way," the dispatcher said. "What were you doing before you started having trouble breathing?" The caller replied, "I was running from the police."

Did you laugh? Life is really funny, even in the chaotic times we live. Laughter is good for the soul and for those around you. It's contagious.

There are no limits to caring ®

October 7

Therefore, since we are surrounded by so great a cloud of witnesses, let us also lay aside every weight and sin which clings so closely, and let us run with endurance the race that is set before us, looking to Jesus, the founder and perfector of our faith (Romans 12:1-2, ESV).

Derek Redmond

At the 1988 Olympic Games, Derek Redmond, a British runner, had to withdraw from the race because of an injury.

Four years later, at the 1992 Olympics, he had another chance and the potential to win a medal. During the race, he pulled into the lead when suddenly he pulled a hamstring and dropped to the ground.

But Derek was determined to finish. Despite the fact that the other runners had already finished the race, he lifted himself back onto his feet and limped down the track.

Derek's father was watching from the stands and ran to his son. He whispered in his ear, "I'm here. We'll finish together." His father wrapped his arms around Derek, and together they finished the race.

When you want to give up because you are hurt, tired, or you've even failed, lean on God and He is always there until the race is finished.

October 8

Be devoted to one another in love. Honor one another above yourselves. Never be lacking in zeal, but keep your spiritual fervor, serving the Lord (Romans 12:10-11, NIV).

Boredom

We spend billions of dollars each year in order to avoid boredom. There's restlessness in the soul, there's a search for meaning, and we try to avoid boredom. But boredom is not so much about amusements as it is relationships.

Sure, we need recreation and entertainment, but what does more to eliminate boredom is relationships. We hunger for a deep and meaningful relationship. And you know what, just as you want friends, so does everyone else.

Why not reach out today with kindness, with friendship, to a new person. Both of you have the potential for a rewarding friendship. Or better yet, invest boredom dollars in the lives of those with needs. Your amusement dollars could turn into a hand up for someone with a special need. Your investment will pay big dividends of joy as you see what you have done.

When you are reaching out to others, you never really have time for boredom.

October 9

Whoever walks with the wise becomes wise, but the companion of fools will suffer harm (Proverbs 13:20, ESV).

Pharaoh

American Pharaoh won the Belmont---becoming the first Triple Crown winner in 37 years and only the 12th horse to ever win the Triple Crown! American Pharaoh was beautiful, gentle, calm, and different than many racehorses.

His owner tried to sell him when he was a stud, but the price was too low! But the owner never gave up.

The trainer had faith and rode with a positive attitude, even though he had just failed three times. And Pharaoh, being surrounded with those positive, determined people, overcame the odds…the circumstances.

Pharaoh was fortunate to have such people around him…we can't always control who is around us…and certainly not their attitude…but we can control or attitude, and if those around us are negative, we can move.

With a can-do attitude…surrounded by people with a can-do spirit…we can win the big races in life.

October 10

They seduce the unstable; they are experts in greed—an accursed breed! (2 Peter 2:14, NIV).

Benedict Arnold

The name Benedict Arnold is synonymous with treason. But he was not always a traitor. During the early years of the Revolutionary War, Arnold was a brave patriot and hero.

But Arnold had been overlooked for military promotions, and he grew frustrated and bitter.

In 1778 he was finally appointed as military governor of Philadelphia, but he used his position to profit from the war and lived extravagantly.

His greed drove him to consorting with British agents, giving them information in exchange for money. He bargained with them for a position as a general in the British army.

Benedict Arnold was driven by greed. And today, still, it is greed that is hurting America, all the way down to the families and individuals that make up this great nation.

Greed will always lead us to places we didn't want to go. Greed will always result in pain, loss, and heartache.

October 11

Therefore a man shall leave his father and mother and hold fast to his wife, and they shall become one flesh (Genesis 2:24, ESV).

Judd

When our son Judd wanted to buy a house, he wondered, would this be a good investment? Would his asset keep its value? The good news is that his asset did increase in value far more than he ever imagined.

Next door to his new home lived a young lady. He liked what he saw. But Judd waited for the right moment before he asked Missy out on a date. A year later, he decided that Missy was the right woman for him, which was affirmed by family and friends as a wise decision. He met with her father and asked for her hand in marriage…a little old-fashioned, but the right way. The next weekend, he proposed marriage, and she said yes.

Take time to find the right person. Cherish your greatest asset, your spouse. Stay close to the one you love, even if the world tumbles in around you. Marriage is a lifetime commitment.

October 12

When the banquet was ready, he sent his servant to tell the guests, "Come, the banquet is ready." But they all began making excuses (Luke 14:17-18, NLT).

Just Do It

During the Spanish-American War, the president desperately needed to contact the leader of the insurgents, General Garcia. Garcia was last known to be fighting somewhere in the mountains of Cuba, but no mail or telegraph could reach him.

An advisor to the president recommended contacting Lieutenant Rowan for help. If anybody could find General Garcia, it would be him. Lieutenant Rowan accepted the job without hesitation. He took the letter, sealed it in a leather pouch, and began his search. He landed in the middle of the night off the coast of Cuba and made his way to the mountains.

After much difficulty, he found General Garcia, delivered the letter, and then headed home.

Lieutenant Rowan didn't ask, "Exactly, where is he?" or "I doubt if I can do it." There was a job to be done, and he did it. Instead of making a dozen excuses why you can't complete the task, just do it. Deliver the goods!

October 13

Let justice roll down like waters, and righteousness like an ever-flowing stream (Amos 5:24, ESV).

Kim Dae Jung.

In 1973, Kim Dae Jung stood blindfolded on the deck of a boat racing through a black midnight sea. His feet were tied to heavy weights. He was moments from death for trying to bring democracy to his country. At the last moment, a U.S. helicopter rescued him.

On Friday, October 13, 2000, Mr. Kim Dae Jung, then President of South Korea, was awarded the Nobel Peace Prize for his pursuit of democracy in South Korea and his efforts to make peace with North Korea.

We may not win the Nobel Peace Prize, but we can work for peace and harmony here in our own community. It takes courage and commitment to work to make our country all it can and should be. There are issues of equality and justice that need voices. You can add your voice and influence toward building up this country.

October 14

Do not forsake your friend and your father's friend
(Proverbs 27:10, ESV).

Good Friend

John Elliott, a forest ranger, was high in the Rocky Mountains and had walked many miles through deep snows. As evening approached, he was exhausted and barely made it back to his cabin as a storm began brewing.

He was so fatigued that he didn't even light a fire or remove his wet clothing. Outside, the blizzard howled, dumping more snow and dropping the temperature rapidly.

Too exhausted to move, John lay freezing on his cabin floor, and he actually began to feel warm all over. He knew that falling asleep would lead to death, but he felt too good to move.

Suddenly, his dog ran to his side and began whining and nudging him, keeping him from falling asleep. Later, John said that if his dog hadn't done that, he would have died.

You all need a friend like that…who looks out for you and won't give up on you.

October 15

People look at the outward appearance, but the LORD looks at the heart (1 Samuel 16:7, NIV).

Thomas Jefferson

While serving as the Vice President, Thomas Jefferson entered one of Baltimore's nicest hotels one evening and asked for a room. However, Jefferson was wearing dirty working clothes, and the hotel manager did not recognize him, so he turned Jefferson away.

Later, the hotel manager discovered Mr. Jefferson's identity, and he hurriedly sent out several employees to find Mr. Jefferson and offer him as many rooms as his heart desired, free of charge.

A hotel employee found Jefferson had booked a room in another hotel, so he presented the manager's offer for rooms free of charge.

But Jefferson refused, asking him to pass this message along to the hotel manager: "I value your hotel's good intentions, but if you have no room for a dirty farmer, then you shall have none for the vice president."

Outward appearances do not determine a person's worth. What you see is not always what's there.

October 16

I am this day eighty-five years old. I am still as strong today as I was in the day that Moses sent me; my strength now is as my strength was then (Joshua 14:10-11, ESV).

Never Too Late

This is a word for those who feel they are over the hill. One of the most prolific and popular writers of this last century was James Mitchener. He is known for works like *Hawaii, Tales from the South Pacific, Centennial,* and many other novels.

Mitchener did not, however, publish a book until he was past 40. Most of his monumental works were done when he was well into the "senior citizen" stage of life. He was working hard on another novel when he died at the age of 90.

How late is "too late" to begin to do what you want to do? Age is as much a state of mind as it is an accumulation of years. Don't let anyone rob you of the joy of making a contribution by telling you that you are too old. You are never too old to make a difference.

October 17

You have been wandering around in this hill country long enough; turn to the north (Deuteronomy 2:3, NLT).

Adjust the Sails

I noticed a sign recently that read, "We can't direct the wind, but we can adjust their sails."

Two ships are at sea: one ship steers east, another west. The same breeze blows for both ships. It is the set of the sail and not the wind that determines the way the ships go.

We are like ships. It is the set of our sails that determines where we will go. Circumstances come and, at times can be very difficult if not devastating. But, by and large, what happens has everything to do with the way we handle the circumstances.

As a result, we can either be bitter or better. We need to deal with our circumstances in a positive way so that our ship can sail where we want to go and not where the wind takes us. Want to change where you are heading? Adjust the sails.

October 18

He turns a desert into pools of water, a parched land into springs of water (Psalm 107:35, ESV).

Charlie Brown

Sparky seemed to fail at everything. He did not do well in school. In the eighth grade, he failed all his subjects. In high school, he flunked physics, Latin, Algebra, and English.

He didn't do much better in sports. He made the school's golf team only to lose the most important match of the season.

He was socially awkward. He probably would have failed at dating, only he never asked anyone to go out with him – he was too afraid of being turned down.

The only thing he thought he did well was draw. He aspired to be a professional artist, only no one seemed to appreciate his drawings. After high school, he sent an application to the Disney studios only to be rejected.

Finally, he decided to tell his story in cartoons…about a little boy failing at everything…he called him Charlie Brown…and the "Peanuts" comic strip was born. Charles Schulz turned losing into great success. What are you doing with your losses?

October 19

If the blind lead the blind, both will fall into a pit
(Matthew 15:14, ESV).

Role Model

President Grover Cleveland had some friends from Vermont as guests for dinner at the White House. However, they did not know which fork to use or what to do. So, they simply followed the lead of the President.

When the coffee was served, the President poured his coffee into his saucer, then put cream and sugar in it. So did his guests. The President then gently set his saucer on the floor – for the cat! At that point, the friends were lost.

Who do you follow? Do you know where you are going? Maybe you need to know before you blindly follow.

But did you know you have the potential to be an excellent role model? As a matter of fact, you are a model.

There are people who are looking up to you and who will follow your lead today. What will you do with your cup and saucer? Think about it.

October 20

The way of a fool is right in his own eyes, but a wise man listens to advice (Proverbs 12:15, ESV).

Advice

Think about this advice:

- Forgive your enemies. It messes up their heads.
- Do not corner something you know is meaner than you.
- Every path has a few puddles.
- When you wallow with pigs, expect to get dirty.
- The best sermons are lived, not preached.
- Most of the stuff people worry about ain't never gonna happen anyway.
- Don't judge folks by their relatives.
- Remember, silence is sometimes the best answer.
- Live a good, honorable life. Then when you get older and think back, you'll enjoy it a second time.
- If you find yourself in a hole, the first thing to do is stop diggin'.
- Lettin' the cat outta the bag is a whole lot easier than puttin' it back in.
- Live simply. Love generously. Care deeply. Speak kindly. Leave the rest up to God.

October 21

I will tear down my barns and build larger ones, and there I will store all my grain and my goods . . . But God said to him, Fool! This night your soul is required of you, and the things you have prepared, whose will they be? (Luke 12:18, 20 ESV).

Stuff

A few years ago we moved into a new house. I could not believe the stuff that I had collected for the past 20 years. Most of the stuff I had not used in years, and yet I was hanging on to all that stuff.

We have a way of accumulating stuff. Then we rent storage buildings to store our stuff, so we can have room to get more stuff, then one day when we are gone, our family can come by and see our stuff and keep the stuff they want and have a garage sale for the other stuff – stuff that nobody ever uses – just stuff to keep.

I did find pictures of friends and family that I had not seen in a while. Strange how we keep stuff and forget about important relationships. Forget the stuff and renew friendships. That's what counts.

October 22

So God created mankind in his own image, in the image of God he created them; male and female (Genesis 1:27, NIV).

Homecoming Queen

It's that time of the year!! Football and Homecoming, Kings and Queens! The excitement of who will be elected to the Homecoming Court.

In Chester, South Dakota, Betsy Daniel was elected Homecoming Queen. So what? Does this sound like the way it goes in thousands of high schools across the country? Betsy is probably different than your typical homecoming queen. She has Down syndrome.

In Lawrence, Kansas, a boy with Down Syndrome was elected to the homecoming court. Luke, a student with autism, was named Homecoming King in 2008.

Could it be that things are changing? Do we now see people as people…not a disability? Do we now see a person with a smile before we see a disability?

There is a possibility that if you live long enough, you too will be a person with a disability. Think about it…would you want to be known for your disability or for who you are?

There are no limits to caring ®

October 23

All the ends of the earth will remember and turn to the LORD, and all the families of the nations will bow down before him (Psalm 22:27, NIV).

Steve Calls

I remember when my wife and I received a phone call from Steve. We like Steve. He dated Katy, our daughter. What he wanted was our blessing to propose to Katy. We gave him our blessing. And would you believe she said, "Yes." Years later, they still have a wonderful marriage.

When Steve asked for our blessing, that was an old tradition. Some modern people wouldn't go there. Traditional family values never go out of style. They make families stronger: traditions like marriage for a lifetime; commitment to one person as the most important person in your life.

Every evening, I watch Canadian geese. They teach traditional family values.

- Canadian geese mate for life.
- They are always together.
- When they have offspring, they share the responsibility of protecting the young and providing food.

Those are the kinds of traditional values that make families strong. There are no limits to caring for your family.

October 24

Whatever one sows, that will he also reap (Galatians 6:7, ESV).

Psychic Hot Line

Linda Maxwell tells about a 10-year-old boy who placed a call to a psychic hotline. The psychic told him four things. The first three are probabilities, and the last one is an absolute certainty.

1. You're going to be rich
2. You're going to be famous
3. You're going to travel around the world.
4. You're going to get into a lot of trouble when your parents see the phone bill for this call.

Not much psychic ability required to make that prediction, is it?

A wise man once said, "The future is but an extension of the present." That's good news, or bad news, depending on what we are doing here and now.

Sowing seeds of hope, love and care in the present will ensure that some of those things will crop up in your future. If you want this kind of harvest in your future, plant some love and care today.

October 25

You lack one thing: go, sell all that you have and give to the poor, and you will have treasure in heaven; and come, follow me (Mark 10:21, ESV).

Mama Stewart

On October 25, 1999, pro-golfer Payne Stewart was killed in a tragic plane crash. Among those left behind was a devoted mother of 81. This petite and definitely spunky lady had always been a positive influence in her son's life.

When Payne won $100,000 in a tournament a few years prior to his death, he donated all of it to a local hospital. When asked about the donation, Payne said his mother told him to do it. When he suggested to her that he give only a portion of it away, she retorted, "If you can't give it all, don't give any of it!"

After her son's death, this little woman decided to run for Congress. She continued to want to give back to her community. She refused to give up, quit trying, or quit living.

When asked about her very small chance of winning, she replied that the outcome was really of no consequence for a mother who already knew what it's like to win…and lose.

October 26

If you pour yourself out for the hungry and satisfy the desire of the afflicted, then shall your light rise in the darkness (Isaiah 58:10, ESV).

Kennedy

John F. Kennedy said, "Ask not what your country can do for you but what you can do for your county."

What if we had accepted his challenge?

The rich and powerful corporations wouldn't have asked for a bailout…they would have said, "What can we do for our county?"

The greedy man would not have asked, "How can I get more…but how can I give more?"

The poor would not have had to ask for help from the government because his neighbor would have already asked, "How can I help you? Here is the food you need and the job for you and your family."

We would not hear much about entitlements…we would hear more about how can I give…not how can I take. We changed Kennedy's challenge to …Ask not what I can do for my county, but what can my country do for me?"

October 27

Be sensitive to each other's needs—don't think of yourself better than others (Romans 12:16, CJB).

Emily Post

Emily Post was a well-to-do society woman. She was married for 13 years when her marriage ended in divorce after Emily discovered her husband's adulterous affairs.

In order to earn extra income, she began writing. And she soon became the expert on etiquette and good manners. Perhaps because of the bad behavior on the part of her husband, Emily Post became driven to tell others how to behave.

So, what is the proper way to hold a fork? It may not be that important because, according to Emily Post, she said that good manners mean having a "sensitive awareness of the feeling of others."

"If you have that awareness," she said, "you have good manners, no matter what fork you use." Be aware of the feelings of those around you. Be kind. That's good manners. Consider the feelings of others …the cashier, your co-worker, your family – now that's good etiquette.

October 28

You yourselves know that these hands of mine have supplied my own needs and the needs of my companions (Acts 20:34, NIV).

Daddy's Birthday

Today would have been my daddy's birthday. He died right before his 87th birthday. He grew up very poor, the son of a sharecropper, 1 of 9 children...who had nothing. When he was 14, his father died, leaving the sharecropping to him. He dropped out of school in the eighth grade and brought in the crops.

When he was 16, he worked in Mobile at the State Docks, and The Coca-Cola Company...was drafted into World War II.

Winning the war and coming home to rebuild the country...Tom Brokoff called this the greatest generation. And my daddy worked hard, married his love who four days earlier turned 17. They had three children and sought to make life better for us and those they met along the way.

After the Korean War, daddy went back to school, became a pastor, principal, educator... From him, I learned compassion, love, and forgiveness.

October 29

For he has rescued us from the kingdom of darkness and transferred us into the kingdom of his dear Son, who purchased our freedom and forgave our sins (Colossians 1:13-14, NLT).

Desks

On the first day of school, Martha, a high school teacher, had all the desks taken out of her classroom. Class began and students walked into a room with no desks. Martha explained, "You can have your desks when you earn them."

This continued with each class throughout the day. Finally, at the end of the day, Martha told her students how to earn their desks.

She opened the door of the classroom, and in walked 27 U.S. veterans, in uniforms, each one carrying a desk. They placed the desks in rows and then stood along the wall.

Martha explained, "You don't have to earn those desks. These guys did it for you. But it's your responsibility to learn, be good students and good citizens, because they paid a price for you to have that desk, and don't ever forget it."

We remembered the men and women who paid the price for our freedom. Today, enjoy that gift of freedom.

October 30

For the happy heart, life is a continual feast (Proverbs 15:15, NLT).

Reducing Stress

More than 30 years ago, *Time* magazine referred to stress as the "The Epidemic of the Eighties" and called it the nation's number one health problem. A survey published in *Prevention* magazine stated that almost 75% of respondents reported that they experienced "great stress" at least one day a week. Up to 90% of visits to primary care practitioners are for problems related to stress.

Do you remember the movie *Patch Adams*? This movie was based on a true story about a physician who practiced medicine with some unusual methods. This doctor used humor and laughter as part of his treatment.

Current scientific research shows that a good laugh is beneficial to the immune system. Laughing also reduces stress hormones. Laughter is the best medicine.

Laughter is one of the cheapest ways to reduce stress. It costs nothing! No equipment. Just laugh!!! The Bible says, "A merry heart is like a good medicine."

October 31

The integrity of the upright guides them, but the unfaithful are destroyed by their duplicity (Proverbs 11:3, NIV).

Masks

Many people are celebrating Halloween this week. Lots of children and adults dress up in masks and costumes to pretend to be someone or something else. A superhero, a princess, a monster. But when Halloween is over, a lot of people are still wearing their masks.

They wear masks to cover up their fears, insecurities, or weaknesses… so that no one sees the real person inside. But, it's actually the masks we wear every day that keep us from developing into everything God created us to be and to developing quality relationships with others.

When we take off our masks, we give God permission to begin to continuously transform us into who He has created us to be. Then we don't have to wear a mask. When we live confidently knowing we are who <u>He</u> says we are, we can be mask-free!

Take off your mask and be who God created you to be!

November 1

The prudent understand where they are going, but fools deceive themselves (Proverbs 14:8, NLT).

Compass

A golfer and a caddie were searching for a golf ball lost deep in the rough. The golfer asked, "Why do you keep looking at that pocket watch?" "It isn't a watch," the caddie said. "It's a compass."

Ever feel like a lost ball in high weeds? At such a time, you need a compass. It may be the need for a moral compass. Some moral issues appear more gray than black or white.

It may be a mental or emotional compass. We can find ourselves confused or emotionally conflicted when dealing with the day-to-day stuff of life.

Where do you find a compass? Try a close friend or family member, a pastor, or respected teacher. Or it could come through prayer.

One thing is sure, we all need a compass from time to time when we can't seem to find our way. Once we find our way, then we can be a compass to others.

November 2

Though he may stumble, he will not fall, for the LORD upholds him with his hand (Psalm 37:24, NIV).

Failure

"I've missed more than 9,000 shots in my career. I've lost almost 300 games. Twenty-six times I've been trusted to take the game-winning shot and missed. I've failed over and over again in my life. And that is why I succeed." No, that's not me. That was Michael Jordan.

What do we do with our failures? Most of us will know more failures than victories. Victory most often has to do with recovering from failure. Getting up after we fall. Keeping on keeping on. Only then can we experience winning.

How we handle failures determines how we deal with life. Our failures need not defeat us. We must keep getting up, and that is the hardest part. Sometimes we need a helping hand so that we can win. Sometimes we can offer a helping hand…who knows, we may be lifting a Michael Jordan.

Today is about getting up and winning.

November 3

Break up your unplowed ground and do not sow among thorns (Jeremiah 4:3, NIV).

Plow Stumps

Paul was a farmer who lived in the 1920s. When he wanted to expand his farm, he had to clear new ground, most of it by hand.

He didn't have tractors. He would cut the trees down, clear the underbrush, and remove a lot of stumps. But he had to decide which stumps to remove and which ones would remain. But some stumps he just could not remove.

When it came time to plant the crop, you could see where Paul had to plow around the stumps. Some stumps he could plow up, but some he had to plow around.

That's the way it is in our lives. We plow around stumps that we cannot plow up. God give me the wisdom to accept the things I cannot change and the courage to change the things I can…and the wisdom to know the difference.

November 4

For you, O God, have heard my vows (Pslam 61:5, ESV).

Wedding Vows

A few weeks before his wedding, the groom approached the minister and offered him $100 to omit the wedding vows where the groom promises to "love, honor and cherish."

The wedding day arrived, and the bride and groom were about to exchange vows. When it came time for the groom's vows, the minister looked at him and said, "Will you promise to humble yourself before her, obey her every wish and command, serve her breakfast in bed every morning and swear that you will never look at another woman, as long as you both shall live?"

The groom whispered to the minister, "I thought we had a deal." The minister put the $100 into his hand and whispered, "She made me a better offer."

What vows did you make on that special day? Take time to do something for your spouse to demonstrate your love…even if it's just breakfast in bed.

November 5

Blessed are the peacemakers, for they will be called children of God (Matthew 5:9, NIV).

Piece-Maker

Katy, a mother of three, woke early one morning to prepare her Sunday School lesson. She wasn't quite finished when her three children began coming downstairs for breakfast.

Katy's children bounded into the kitchen, looking through the refrigerator and cabinets for something to eat. They soon found a box of toaster pastries with only one pastry remaining. They all began screaming and fighting, each claiming the pastry.

Katy finished writing the Bible verse, "Blessed are the peacemakers for they shall be called sons of God."

Attempting to quiet her children, Katy said, "Would somebody PLEASE be the peacemaker?!" There was a moment of silence, and then her oldest child said, "I'll be the piece maker, Mom!" He then took the pastry and began breaking it into pieces for his siblings, saying, "Here's a piece for you, a piece for you, and a piece for me."

Peacemaker? Few have learned the art of peacemaking. Make peace today with yourself and one another.

There are no limits to caring ®

November 6

It is better to finish something than to start it (Ecclesiastes 7:8, NCV).

Lincoln

Abraham Lincoln was not a handsome person! Before the election of 1860, an eleven-year-old girl, Grace Bedell, first wrote Lincoln in October that she thought he would look better with "whiskers" and he would get more votes.

Republicans in New York later wrote he would be "much improved in appearance" if he were to grow whiskers…

Most of the pictures we see of Lincoln have a beard. Two thoughts:

First, I think it is interesting that an 11-year-old girl could have that kind of influence over such a great man. No matter how young you are, you can make a difference.

Second, Lincoln finished his life with a beard. And it's how we best remember him. Finish well…for that is the lasting impression. How you finish makes the difference!

Listen to children and finish well! Children will teach you much and how you finish will probably be remembered more than how you started!

November 7

Give me now wisdom and knowledge (2 Chronicles 1:10, ESV).

The Secret of Life

A little boy looked up at an older man, "I understand you're a very wise man. I'd like to know the secret of life."

The old man looked down at the youngster and replied: "I've thought a lot in my lifetime, and the secret can be summed up in four words:

"The first is think. Think about the values you wish to live your life by.

"The second is believe. Believe in yourself based on the thinking you've done about the values you're going to live your life by.

"The third is dream. Dream about the things that can be, based on your belief in yourself and the values you're going to live by.

"The last is dare. Dare to make your dreams become reality based on your belief in yourself and your values."

And with that, Walter E. Disney said to the little boy, "Think, Believe, Dream, and Dare."

There are no limits to caring ®

November 8

I urge, then, first of all, that petitions, prayers, intercession, and thanksgiving be made for all people— for kings and all those in authority (1 Timothy 2:1-2, NIV).

After the Election

History has been made! You may or may not agree with the outcome of the elections. But more important, it is time to support those who have been elected to lead our great nation, as well as those elected to serve us right here at home.

How do we support?

First, we support by praying for wisdom, strength, and accountability for our President-elect and all of our elected. That is our responsibility as good citizens.

Second, we must unite. We have been divided far too long. We need to come together as one…United States of America.

The divisiveness in this country that we have seen in our lifetime will ultimately destroy us. We must work for the common good of all, or there will be nothing for anyone.

Now is the time to pray and unite. And we can do both even if we don't always agree.

November 9

And I will break down the wall that you have smeared with whitewash and bring it down to the ground (Ezekiel 13:14, ESV).

Walls

November 9, 1989, is when the wall dividing communist East Germany from West Germany crumbled. For 28 years, this wall was a symbol of repression. Many people were prisoners in their own country.

The fall of the wall sent shockwaves around the world that night, abruptly ending the Cold War and paving the way for the fall of the Soviet Union.

Reagan's Quote: "Today we have too many walls that divide…divide us from talking, that keep us from loving and caring for each other."

We find walls in churches, government, work, and family. We must tear down walls that divide…walls built out of fear and a need to control.

What about in your own family. Are there walls that separate you from other family members? Maybe you could hammer away at tearing down your wall.

There are no limits to caring ®

November 10

Your old men shall dream dreams, and your young men shall see visions (Joel 2:28, ESV).

Albert's Dream

My friend Albert has this dream of one day being a linebacker for the New York Jets. This has been a lifelong dream. My concern is that my friend is 5'6" and only weighs 120 lbs. soaking wet. He is also 45. This is not a realistic dream.

It doesn't hurt to dream the impossible, but we need also to dream the possible - things that can be achieved. Albert won't ever be a linebacker for the Jets. If he grows another foot and adds a couple hundred pounds, maybe…but not likely!

When our dreams fade, we need new dreams that are realistic. Dreams are important. We shouldn't take them lightly, but when dreams take us away from reality, we have to find new dreams, new hopes, new directions.

Albert might do better to dream of being a jockey at the Kentucky Derby than a linebacker for the Jets.

November 11

You know the way to the place where I am going (John 14:4, NIV).

Knowing Where I'm Going

You probably know this riddle and may even know the answer. "As I was going to St. Ives, I met a man with seven wives. Every wife had seven sacks, and every sack had seven cats, and every cat had seven kittens. Kittens, cats, sacks, and wives, how many were going to St. Ives?" If you multiply, you'll come up with 2800, but if you're smart, you know the answer is only one.

The person in the riddle knew where he was going. Regardless of others, he was going to St. Ives. It's good to know where you are going.

If you get to where you are going, where will that be? Will it be where you want to be? It helps to know your destination, and it's even better if it is someplace you want to go.

Wherever you go, there will always be people who need you to demonstrate there are no limits to caring.

November 12

You are just a vapor that appears for a little while and then vanishes away (James 4:14, ESV).

Enjoy Every Sandwich

Lee Lipthensal was a physician, teacher, and director of the Preventative Medicine Research Institute in California. When he was diagnosed in 2009 with terminal esophageal cancer, he began writing a book titled, *Enjoy Every Sandwich*. While undergoing treatments, he was determined to make the most of each day and be at peace with his fate.

When asked if he had anything he wanted to do before he died, Lee replied that he didn't need to travel to exotic countries or jump out of planes. He had lived his life loving others, and he had no regrets.

Lee and his family had hoped for a miracle, but he passed away in 2011, leaving behind a legacy to practice gratitude, love others, live each day to the fullest, and enjoy every sandwich.

Love and appreciate others and let them know it because you don't know which day will be your last.

November 13

My days are swifter than a runner; they flee away (Job 9:25, ESV).

BREVITY OF TIME

Life passes very quickly. An unknown poet wrote:

When as a child I laughed and wept,
>Time crept.
>>When as a youth, I dreamed and talked,
>>>Time walked.
>>>>When I became a full-grown man,
>>>>>Time ran.
>>>>>>When older still I grew,
>>>>>>>Time flew.
>>>>>>>>Soon I shall find in traveling on,
>>>>>>>>>Time gone.

Because of the brevity of time, each day is packed with significance. Today is the time for building relationships with our children. Today is the time for expressing love for our mates. Today is the time for dealing with our bad habits and creating some good habits.

Someone has said, "Yesterday is a canceled check. Tomorrow is a promissory note. Only today is legal tender." That being true, make it a great day. Make it count by investing in those relationships that really matter.

There are no limits to caring ®

November 14

Children are a heritage from the LORD, offspring a reward from him (Psalm 127:3, NIV).

Kids and the Bible

Here are some of the things children learned in Sunday School:
- In the first book of the Bible, Genesis, God got tired of creating the world, so he took the Sabbath off.
- Adam & Eve were created from an apple tree.
- The first commandment was when Eve told Adam to eat the apple.
- Noah's wife was called Joan of Ark.
- Moses led the Hebrews to the Red Sea, where they made unleavened bread, which is bread made without any ingredients.
- The Egyptians were all drowned in the desert.
- Afterward, Moses went up on Mount Cyanide to get the Ten Amendments.
- The Fifth Commandment is to humor thy mother and father.
- When Moses died, Joshua led the Hebrews in the Battle of Geritol.
- Solomon had 300 wives and 700 porcupines.
- A Christian should have only one wife. This is called monotony.

November 15

But God has so composed the body, giving greater honor to the part that lacked it (1 Corinthians 12:24, ESV).

Jamie Scott

Jamie was trying out for a part in the school play. He had his heart set on being in the play and was really excited about auditioning for one of the lead roles.

Jamie's mom was afraid he would be upset if he didn't land the lead role. On the day the parts were awarded, she went to pick him up from school.

Jamie rushed up to his mom, eyes shining with pride and excitement. "Guess what, Mom," he shouted, and then said amazing words..."I've been chosen to clap and cheer."

Maybe we don't all hold places that the world considers prestigious. But no matter our position in life, each of us play a part in life that is vital, unique, and important...whether you are a parent, a friend, an employee.

Whenever you are disappointed with your place in life or your circumstances have you down, stop and think about little Jamie Scott and find joy in your day.

November 16

I will set shepherds over them who will care for them
(Jeremiah 23:4, ESV).

Bumper Stickers

Several years ago, *The Washington Post* judged the following bumper stickers among the best:

- Love May Be Blind, But Marriage Is A Real Eye Opener.
- The Trouble With The Gene Pool Is That There Is No Life Guard.
- I'm Going To Graduate On Time, No Matter How Long It Takes.
- If You Want Breakfast In Bed, Sleep In The Kitchen.
- Old Age Comes At A Bad Time.
- Where There's A Will, I Want To Be In It.
- If At First You Don't Succeed, Skydiving Isn't For You.
- What If The Hokey Pokey Is Really What It's All About?
- First Things First, But Not Necessarily In That Order.
- Consciousness: That Annoying Time Between Naps.
- As Long As There Are Tests, There Will Be Prayer In School.
- Always Remember, You're Unique, Just Like Everyone Else

We have our own bumper sticker. It reads: There are no limits to caring.

November 17

If anyone is not willing to work, let him not eat (2 Thessalonians 3:10, ESV).

Little Red Hen

Remember The Little Red Hen? She shared a cottage with a gossiping goose, a vain cat, and a lazy dog.

One day the little red hen found some grains of wheat. "Who will help me plant them?" she asked. No takers. Later she asked, "Who will help me harvest the grain?" No takers. Later, "who will help me grind the grain?" Still, no takers. "Who will help me make dough?" Her trio of friends all had other things to do. "Who will help me bake it into bread?" They all had their excuses.

When she took the bread out of the oven, she asked, "Now, who will help me eat it?" They all volunteered, "I will!" Well, you know the story. She said, in effect, "No, I did the work. I will enjoy the benefits!" So, she ate the bread.

Not much has changed. Those who do the work usually enjoy the benefits.

November 18

A time to be silent and a time to speak (Ecclesiastes 3:7, NIV).

Stumpy

Every year Stumpy wanted to ride in the airplane at the state fair. Martha would always say, "That ride costs ten dollars, and ten dollars is ten dollars." This year Stumpy said, "I'm 78. I may never get another chance." Martha replied, "Stumpy, that ride costs ten dollars, and ten dollars is ten dollars."

The pilot, hearing the conversation, offered them a deal. He said, "I will fly you both for free if you can stay quiet for the entire ride. If you say one word, it's full price." They agreed and up they went.

The pilot did all his twists, turns, and rolls trying to rattle them. Not one word. Finally, he landed and said, "I did everything I could to get you to yell out, but you didn't." Stumpy replied, "Well, I wanted to say something back up there when Martha fell out, but ten dollars is ten dollars.

Sometimes, what we preach has a way of coming home at the wrong time.

November 19

Give us this day our daily bread (Matthew 6:11, ESV).

Yesterday, Tomorrow

Have you ever considered that yesterday and tomorrow exist only in your mind? You are completely powerless to change yesterday or tomorrow. The only period of time you have any power over is now.

Yesterday exists only in your memory. Its effect on you lingers only in the space in your mind that you allocate to it.

Tomorrow is a question mark. You may not even be here. Or you could win one million dollars and tomorrow could take a radically different course. Maybe, maybe not.

The one part of time in which you have measure of control is right now! You can respond to the events in your life in a positive manner, which will ensure peace and happiness for yourself and others, or you can make choices that will create the opposite effect. Right now is yours. What will you do with it?

There are no limits to caring ®

November 20

[God] sent his Son as an atoning sacrifice . . . since God so loved us, we also ought to love one another (1 John 4:10-11, NIV).

Kidney

Debbie Stoudimere's younger brother has been a diabetic since he was 18 months old. These 50 years of insulin reactions have destroyed his kidneys. A kidney transplant was his only chance.

After searching for a match, tests showed that Debbie was a 10 out of 10 match.

Even though the risk was great, Debbie gave one of her kidneys to her brother. Debbie didn't hesitate to make this sacrifice...she knew the price and was willing to pay the price to give. One gave so that another might live.

Before the surgery, Debbie said she was not fearful, "God has had his hands upon us. The Lord led us this far, and He will not let us down."

Debbie said, "My brother is a good man. He would have done the same for me. Except for the grace of God, there too I go."

For Debbie, there are no limits to caring.

November 21

The righteous is generous and gives (Psalm 37:21, ESV).

Ice Cream Sundae

A ten-year-old boy entered a hotel coffee shop and sat at a table. "How much is an ice cream sundae?" he asked a waitress. "Fifty cents," she replied. The little boy pulled his hand out of his pocket and studied his coins.

"Well, how much is a plain dish of ice cream?" By this time, more customers were waiting for a table, and the waitress was impatient. "Thirty-five cents," she said abruptly. Counting his coins once more, the little boy decided on the plain ice cream. The waitress brought it out, put the bill on the table, and walked away.

When the boy finished, he paid the cashier and left. The waitress came back to wipe down the table, and she began to cry. There, placed neatly beside the empty dish, was fifteen cents. You see, he couldn't have the sundae because he had to have enough left to leave her a tip.

There are no limits to caring ®

November 22

This also is vanity and a striving after wind (Ecclesiastes 4:4, ESV).

Digging a Hole

There were two guys working for a city. One would dig, dig, dig a hole, and the other would come behind him and fill, fill, fill the hole. These two men worked diligently. One digging a hole, the other filling it up again.

A man watched from the sidewalk. He saw how hard these men were working but couldn't understand what they were doing. He finally had to ask them.

He walked over and said to the hole digger, "I appreciate how hard you work, but what are you guys doing? You dig a hole, and your partner comes behind you and fills it up again!"

The hole digger looked at him and replied, "Oh yeah, it must look funny, but the guy who plants the trees is out sick today."

When there's a change in our life, we can't keep on doing it the way we've always done it. We gotta be smart.

November 23

All these blessings will come upon you and accompany you if you obey the LORD your God (Deuteronomy 28:2, NIV).

Receiving God's Blessings

How do you receive blessings from God? The Lord's Prayer that many of us know by memory may offer a clue.... clues that will change your life and give you blessings from God. God is not someone to be manipulated, put in a box, or serve as our personal genie.

But he does want to bless each of us, but sometimes we do more to block His blessings than He can overcome.

Receiving blessings has everything to do with our attitude and behavior. Too much energy is spent on the negatives,
- how to get even with those who have wronged you—
- finding out what's wrong with the world,
- and spending a day and night spreading the bad news or creating bad news.

When we live in such a negative thought process, we will block every positive blessing from coming our way. Sometimes we must change before God can bless us.

There are no limits to caring ®

November 24

My honesty will testify for me (Genesis 30:33, NIV).

Thanksgiving Turkey

It was the day before Thanksgiving, and Jim realized that he had forgotten to buy a turkey. He headed to the butcher shop and got there just as it was closing up.

Jim pleaded with the butcher to let him in. "I forgot to buy a turkey, and my wife will kill me if I don't come home with one!" So the butcher grudgingly opened the door and went to check the freezer. There was only one scrawny turkey left.

The butcher brought it out to show Jim. "That one is too skinny. What else do you have?" The butcher took the bird back into the freezer and waited a few minutes. Then he brought the same turkey out to Jim.

Jim thought for a moment, "That one doesn't look any better. You better give me both of them."

Honesty is always the better choice. Better choice for a salesman, better choice for a husband, better choice for each of us.

November 25

Oh give thanks to the LORD (1 Chronicles 16:8, ESV).

Thanksgiving

What a beautiful month! Fall weather, beautiful landscape, a season of caring and thanksgiving. Each day, give thanks to God for at least three things in your life.

Thanksgiving is comprised of two words… thanks and giving. We are to be thankful AND give. Give to others, your community, your church, your faith group. When the Pilgrims arrived in New England, they were unprepared for the life ahead. A Native American tribe in that region helped the Pilgrims learn to plant corn, hunt, and fish. Because of this, the Pilgrims were saved from starvation.

Out of the Pilgrims came THANKS for what the Native Americans did for them. They GAVE by sharing a feast with the native tribe. As one can see from this story, it began with thanks and naturally turned to giving. Giving thanks always raises our spirits.

November 26

Whoever pursues righteousness and kindness will find life, righteousness, and honor (Proverbs 21:21, ESV).

Acts of Kindness

Rabbi Harold Kushner said, "When you give and carry out acts of kindness, it's as though something inside your body responds and says, 'Yes, this is how I ought to feel.'" That statement is echoed by a group of people who saw a need and acted.

Mrs. Betty, an 82-year-old lady, entered her insurance agent's office to pay her monthly house insurance. During the conversation at the office, the employees asked Betty about her plans for Thanksgiving. Betty replied that she had no family, and since finances were scarce, she would not be having a Thanksgiving meal.

Upon further investigation, the employees learned that Betty was using her last Social Security dollars to pay for her house insurance, and there was no money for food. In addition, she had no fuel for her heater.

The employees went into action, and by the end of the day, Betty had food and fuel and something in the employee's soul was saying, "Yes, this is how we ought to feel."

November 27

Be diligent in these matters; give yourself wholly to them so that everyone may see your progress (1 Timothy 4:15, NIV).

Grandmother Flying

My grandmother was 74 the first time she flew. I had arranged for her to fly with me on a twin-engine plane. The day was beautiful, but my grandmother was rather anxious.

Shortly after take-off, she had the courage to look out the window. She responded, "Why have we stopped up here?" From her vantage point, she thought we had stopped in midair, but we were moving about 200 mph.

Sometimes we think we are not making progress, but we're doing more than just standing still. Like raising a family – changing diapers - trying to instill values – trying to teach the right way – seems like sometimes we are at a standstill – not progressing.

Day by day, progress is made, and our responsibility is to keep on when it seems like we are stuck and can't move.

By doing good and being faithful to what is right, we really are moving much faster than we know.

November 28

Do not judge by appearances, but judge with right judgment (John 7:24, ESV).

Broccoli

A farmer bought some vegetables to plant a garden. He made sure to include his favorite- broccoli.

The farmer placed the vegetables in the ground and realized he had one broccoli plant left, so he placed it in the back. Soon the garden began to flourish – all except that one broccoli plant.

He tried everything. More fertilizer, more water… less fertilizer, less water – nothing helped. He gave up. When summer ended, he went to pull up the dried-up okra stalks and tomato vines, he came across that broccoli – covered with Brussels Sprouts!

Somehow a Brussels sprout got mixed in the broccoli set. All summer he had thought there was something wrong with the plant. But it had been growing the entire time.

Like the farmer, do you ever make the wrong assumption about a person or circumstance and try to change them? Often, they don't need to be fixed but rather given time to sprout.

November 29

There is one Lord, one faith, one baptism, one God and Father of all (Ephesians 4:5-6, NLT).

One

Recently a resident in one of our group homes for the developmentally disabled passed away. At the funeral service, a resident from the home stood and sang, "We are one in the Spirit, we are one in the Lord."

Not only was it touching to see and hear this tribute in song, but in that setting it also rang so true! When it comes to the basic issues of life and death, we are truly one. Whether we are able or disabled, whether we are strong or weak, whether we are rich or poor, whether we are young or old. In that setting, in that funeral home chapel, all were on equal footing. All grieved together, and all recognized a common humanity.

Having a sense of unity or oneness doesn't mean that we are not different. It means that there is more that binds us together than separates us. That is also true for our country. "For we are one in the Spirit" in these challenging times.

November 30

Teach them to your children, talking about them when you sit at home and when you walk along the road, when you lie down and when you get up (Deuteronomy 11:19, NIV).

Better to Give

Lori picked up her 7-year-old son from school. As they always did, the mother began to quiz her son about what he had learned in school that day. In his unique way, he said, "Mom, did you know it is better to give than it is to receive?" That's what he had learned! And he wanted to make sure his mom knew it too!

Like most moms, she learned that long ago—and a wonderful conversation happened between a mother and a son—on giving something that some never learn.

Most of the important things we have learned by 7, or we miss them. Things like:
- Be kind to one another
- Do unto others as you would have them do to you.
- It is better to give than to receive.

The beauty of raising children is when we see such values lived out in the way we treat one another.

December 1

My power is made perfect in weakness (2 Corinthians 12:9, ESV).

People with Disabilities

My sister has an intellectual disability. She was with me the other day and pointed out to me when she saw a blind man pushing a wheelchair across a busy, four-lane road. Sitting in that wheelchair was a man who only had one leg.

That's amazing. One had eyes; one had legs. And one had the ability to see that this was an interesting way for people with disabilities to work together.

People with disabilities have often been looked down upon, discounted. But in God's eyes, they are just as precious as us.

In fact, some of our great leaders have been people with disabilities: Helen Keller, Franklin Roosevelt, Senator Bob Dole, Congressman Tony Coehlo, Governor David Paterson.

Don't discount others because of their differences or weaknesses. Instead, see them as the beautiful people they are, who are overcoming obstacles every day, obstacles that many of us will never have to endure.

December 2

In my former book, Theophilus, I wrote about all that Jesus began to do and to teach (Acts 1:1, NIV).

Worth Catching

Well it's that time again – Colds, viruses, and flus are going around. Kids are staying home—passing around the bug to anyone with an open mouth! People are calling in sick to work.

When my wife gets sick, I know exactly how to take care of her. She has shown me how whenever I'm under the weather. By her example, I know what she wants and how to take care of her.

We learn compassion best when we experience it and spread it to others. It is contagious – but believe me, it's worth catching! And once you've had it you will always want it. That is Love and compassion!

Jesus taught us by example. And we are to treat one another just as he has treated us. Jesus said, "When you have done it to the least of these, you have done it unto me." He truly showed us There are no limits to caring.

December 3

May the God of hope fill you with all joy and peace
(Romans 15:13, NIV).

Hope/Help

Years ago, I recall how I would often be confused by the word, *hoped*. I would hear older adults say, "Mr. Jones came by and hoped me with my chores or hoped me with my harvest." I thought he should have used the word help, "He came by and helped." But he used the word *hoped*.

Nowadays, *hoped* is not used for the word helped. But I think *hoped* caught a concept that we missed. For when we come by to help someone with a chore or project, we really do more than just help. We give hope.

By helping, the task is moved toward completion, and the friend has a new feeling of hope. We all need hope. Without hope, we can't do anything. With hope we can move mountains. Look and see that person who needs you to *hope* them today!

There are no limits to caring ®

December 4

Remember the Sabbath day, to keep it holy (Exodus 20:8, ESV).

Eric Liddell

Eric Henry Liddell participated in the 1924 Olympic Games held in Paris. He was the favorite to win the 100-meter sprint. However, he never won that race.

Why? Months before the games, he learned that the qualifying run would be held on Sunday. He refused to violate his commitment of keeping the Sabbath as the Lord's Day. He took himself out of the competition and began training for the 400- meter races. His friends tried to persuade Liddell to make an exception to his commitment and principles, but he refused.

He trained for the 400-meter run. Just before the race, a trainer gave him a Bible verse. "I will honor those who honor me." This verse was part of the inspiration that caused Liddell to not only win the race but to set a new Olympic record for the 400-meter race.

You always win big when you keep your commitments to God.

December 5

Be strong and courageous. Do not be afraid or discouraged (2 Chronicles 32:7, NIV).

Nelson Mandela

Nelson Mandela was imprisoned for many years for leading the fight against apartheid in South Africa.

Shortly after Mandela was released from jail, he and some friends were flying in a small plane when the propeller suddenly stopped turning. Everyone began to panic until they noticed that Mandela was remaining very calm. This had a calming effect on all the passengers.

When the plane safely landed, Mandela turned to his friend and said, "You know, I was scared up there."

In prison, Mandela had learned that the more you behave as if you're not afraid, the less afraid you become. He had learned that to become courageous, you must act courageously.

Are you facing something in your life that requires courage? Courage is not the absence of fear. In fact, fear must be present for courage to exist. Courage keeps us going. Without it, we give up! What we stand for is lost. Courage is what we all need today.

December 6

Rejoice and be glad, for your reward is great in heaven
(Matthew 5:12, ESV).

Rewards

One afternoon, in the bustle of Christmas shopping, a lady lost her handbag. It was found a few hours later by an honest little boy and returned to her.

Looking in her purse, the lady commented, "Hmmm... That's funny. When I lost my bag, there was a $20 bill in it. Now there are twenty $1 bills."

The boy quickly replied, "That's right, lady. The last time I found a lady's purse, she didn't have any change for a reward."

We all like to get rewarded for the good things we do. At Volunteers of America, we have many opportunities for you to give a gift that will help others. Your reward will be knowing that you've helped someone in need this holiday season.

You can give a warm blanket to someone who can't afford to pay a high heating bill. Or you can collect food for the needy. Whatever your gift, know that your reward is helping others.

December 7

Do not withhold good from those to who it is due when it is in your power to act (Proverbs 3:27, NIV).

Pearl Harbor

On this date, December 7, 1941, 353 Japanese warplanes attacked the U.S. Pacific fleet at Pearl Harbor. It took only 110 minutes for the attackers to sink every battleship in Pearl Harbor, killing 2,403 service people, wounding 1,178, with 640 missing in action.

President Roosevelt called it "a date that will live in infamy!" That attack propelled the United States into World War II.

Thomas Jefferson said, "The price of freedom is eternal vigilance." Pearl Harbor caught our service men and women, and our nation, off guard. As a consequence, "preparedness" has been a watchword of our Military.

We pause today to remember the sacrifice of those brave men and women, and the hundreds of thousands who would later follow them in the defense of our nation.

They truly demonstrated There are no limits to caring– love for our country, for our freedom, and for our families. We honor them, and in so doing, remind ourselves that freedom is costly.

December 8

The heartfelt counsel of a friend is as sweet as perfume and incense (Proverbs 27:9, NLT).

Unlikely Friends

The December 2004 tsunami killed thousands of people and displaced millions in Southeast Asia. But the devastating effects were not only felt just by humans.

When the tsunami struck, a wild baby hippopotamus was washed away from his herd. He was orphaned. The following day, nearby villagers found him and brought him to a local wildlife park.

But he needed a surrogate parent. So, the search began…and ended at the unlikeliest of animals. A 130-year-old giant turtle befriended and adopted the frightened hippo.

The old turtle, who was a cranky loner, formed a tight bond with the baby hippo. The two began eating together and sleeping side by side. More than two years later, the hippo still follows that old turtle around the park.

Don't let your differences get in the way of loving. Acceptance is everything. And by the way, this turtle didn't get too old – or too hard to learn to love and care.

December 9

Get wisdom, get understanding; do not forget my words or turn away from them (Proverbs 4:5, NIV).

Kirk Douglas

Veteran actor Kirk Douglas had a debilitating stroke that left him unable to speak. In his efforts at recovery, he discovered some guidelines that he said should be helpful in dealing with any sickness or misfortune.

- WHEN THINGS GO BAD, always remember: It could be worse.
- NEVER, NEVER GIVE UP. Keep working on your speech – and your life.
- NEVER LOSE YOUR SENSE OF HUMOR. Laugh at yourself, laugh with others.
- STEM DEPRESSION by thinking of, reaching out to, and helping others.
- DO UNTO OTHERS as you would have them do unto you.
- PRAY, not for God to cure you, but to help you help yourself.

These are good practical ways of dealing with difficulty. They worked for Kirk Douglas. He recovered enough to star in a movie that dealt with a stroke victim. Don't give up. Keep the faith.

December 10

Let the wise hear and increase in learning (Proverbs 1:5, ESV).

College Education

A college education need not be a dream. If you want to go to college, you can make it a reality.

At 24 years of age, he had finished the eighth grade. He and his dad had both been sharecroppers. His dad died. He knew only poverty, but at 24, he had a dream of going to college.

With effort and determination, he managed to enroll in college and went on to obtain three degrees. He is my dad, and through the years, he encouraged young and old alike to continue their education. In fact, he helped make it possible for numerous students to go to college.

Where there's a will, there's a way! Make your dreams a reality, for there is a way. If you have a dream of a college education or training, it is possible. Call a local college, university, or call me. You may find this dream achievable. You could even get started this January.

December 11

A stingy man hastens after wealth and does not know that poverty will come upon him (Proverbs 28:22, ESV).

Cheap Gifts

Tom had been away on a business trip right before Christmas. He still needed to buy his wife a gift.

So he went to a nearby mall and approached the perfume counter. "How much does this perfume cost?" he asked the sales clerk. She showed him the price tag – $50.

"Do you have anything smaller?" Tom asked. The sales clerk returned with a smaller bottle for $30. "That's still a bit too expensive," he said. Growing aggravated, the clerk brought out a tiny $15 bottle of perfume.

Impatiently Tom said, "What I mean is that I'd like to see something real cheap." So, the clerk handed him a mirror.

With the current economy, we will all be cutting back on gifts this year. But it's not a matter of how much you spend. Rather, it's how you show how much you care. The perfect gift is your heart. Give it, and all else comes naturally.

December 12

God settles the solitary in a home (Psalm 68:6, ESV).

Safe House

December 12, 1899, a young Winston Churchill scaled a 10-foot wall and escaped from a South African military prison. After wandering for several days and feeling totally exhausted, he decided to approach a home where he saw lights shining through a window.

Although there was a price on his head, he felt he had to take a chance of finding a friendly home in the heart of enemy country.

He prayed earnestly that he be guided to the right house. When he knocked on the door, a man opened it and asked Churchill what he wanted. He replied, "I'm Winston Churchill." "Come in," a friendly voice said. "This is the only house for miles around where you would be safe."

Being in a safe house and a safe environment is so important. We call this place "home." A place where we are loved and have a sense of safety.

December 13

Teach us to number our days (Psalm 90:12, NIV).

My Last Day

Steve Jobs had a unique morning ritual since he was 17 years old. Every morning, he would look in the mirror and ask this question: "If today were the last day of my life, would I want to do what I am about to do today?"

A few years ago, he was diagnosed with pancreatic cancer. With the certainty of a rapidly approaching death, Steve's morning reflection on his last day on earth became a real possibility.

What if today was your last day? What would you do? Would you be kinder, more gracious to others?

What unfinished business do you have? With your children, spouse or parents? Would you need to tell someone "I love you," or "I'm sorry," or "You've been a blessing to me, thanks"?

Live each day as if it's your last, and you find meaning for this day.

December 14

[The LORD gives] beauty for ashes (Isaiah 61:3, NKJV).

Beethoven

Beethoven lived much of his life in fear of deafness. Being a famous composer and pianist, he was concerned because he believed that the sense of hearing was vital to creating music.

When Beethoven discovered that he was indeed losing his hearing, he was almost overcome with anxiety. He consulted doctors and tried every possible remedy. But the deafness increased until, at last, all of his hearing was gone.

Despite his hearing loss and the possibility of the end of his career, Beethoven continued in his music. And to everyone's astonishment, he wrote some of his greatest music after he became totally deaf.

His deafness became a great asset. He was able to use his weakness, his handicap, to become an even greater musician. He did not allow it to defeat him.

Don't let your weakness stop you. Let God turn your weaknesses into beautiful music.

December 15

You must be compassionate, just as your Father is compassionate (Luke 6:36, NLT).

Tolstoy – War and Peace

In the book *War and Peace,* the story is told of a rather rich society lady. She attended a play one evening and was moved to tears by the actors on stage.

It was a cold night, and while she sat in the comforts of the theater, her buggy driver sat in the cold. When she returned to her buggy, she found that her driver had frozen to death. She complained because she would have to wait for another driver to take her home.

We may be moved to tears by what we see at theaters, plays, and movies, but what should really concern us is the buggy driver who freezes to death.

At the real theater of life, compassion put in action makes a difference in a person's life. Look around today and you will see someone who needs your act of compassion. Don't complain; express compassion with action…there are no limits to caring.

December 16

Fear not (Matthew 10:31, ESV).

Fear

President Roosevelt said, "The only thing we have to fear is fear itself." He was speaking to the nation, to the world, during the time of WWII. Would we win the war, or would we lose the war? The answer was very uncertain. But President Roosevelt knew that if we let fear control us, we would lose the war and everything.

Don't let fear control you. Don't replace compassion with fear. You may fear, but don't let fear control our efforts to do good to one another.

The spirit of fear and timidity does not come from God. 2 Timothy 1:7 says, "For God has not given us a spirit of fear, but of power and of love and of a sound mind."

If you begin to feel fear, focus on the positive in the situation or have a good laugh about it. Embrace your desire to do good to one another and FEAR NOT!

December 17

Love is patient and kind; love does not envy or boast (1 Corinthians 13:4, ESV).

Tasmanian Devil

Do you know the popular Tasmanian devil cartoon that leaves a path of destruction in his wake? But real Tasmanian devils are actually similar to the cartoon. They are loud and aggressive, tough and strong.

When they feed, they compete with each other to protect their share of the food. They screech and squeal and bite each other's faces. The mating process is violent too. The males fight over the females, and the winner grabs the female by the neck and drags her back to his den.

But the real Tasmanian devils are becoming endangered. Why? They are dying of cancer, tumors on their faces. And when they bite each other's faces, it spreads the disease. They are becoming endangered because of the way they treat each other!

We, too, may be endangered because of the way we treat one another. Don't spread the disease of hate, aggression, or violence. Instead, spread love and kindness…that's a daily choice. There are no limits to caring.

December 18

Above all, keep loving one another earnestly, since love covers a multitude of sins (1 Peter 4:8, ESV).

Ugly Dog

A lady sought to find a home for an ugly stray dog. Her rural home was a popular place for people to drop off unwanted pets, but this particular dog presented a real challenge because the dog was so ugly. She finally placed an ad in the newspaper saying, "Ugly, but loving little dog. Free to a good home."

She started getting calls immediately. An elderly couple drove up. The man picked the dog up, took her over to the passenger window of his car where his wife sat.

The little dog leaped from the man's arms into the woman's lap. With a look of adoration, the dog laid her head on the woman's shoulder.

The man said, "We'll take her." The lady who placed the ad said, "I didn't realize there was such a market for ugly." The man responded, "It's not the ugly there's a market for. It's the loving. There's always a market for 'love – There are no limits to caring.

December 19

Be patient, then, brothers and sisters (James 5:7, NIV).

Mandy Expecting

When our daughter Mandy was a young child, she always had difficulties waiting for Christmas to open her gifts. She has been known to open a gift and then rewrap it! The suspense was just too much!

As an expecting mother, she was confronted with a gift that she could not open early. She wanted to hurry and open this gift…maybe rewrap it…or just get it early. Mandy was ready for her son to be born months before he was ready!

I reminded her…in "the fullness of time." She didn't like that phrase when she was heavy with child, a very special gift from God.

What every child needs is patience. Sometimes, we're in a hurry…we've got other priorities, but the child just needs patience.

We all need a little patience…with ourselves, with those we live with, and those we work with. Patience is carrying the load you wish you didn't have at the moment.

There are no limits to caring ®

December 20

For I know the plans I have for you, declares the LORD, plans to prosper you and not to harm you, plans to give you hope and a future (Jeremiah 29:11, ESV).

Rudolph

One December night, in a drafty two-bedroom apartment, Bob May and his daughter sat staring out the window.

The little girl, sobbing, "Daddy, why isn't mommy just like everybody else's mommy?" Bob's wife had cancer and had been too weak to come home. He struggled to give hope to his child. He also couldn't afford to buy Christmas. Instead, he made a storybook!

Slowly he began, "Once upon a time, there was a reindeer named Rudolph, and he had a big shiny red nose. People teased him and called him Rudolph the Red-Nosed Reindeer."

As Bob continued, he tried to communicate to his daughter that, even though some of God's creatures are different, they are still special. You see, Rudolph's character was an outcast same way Bob was growing up…

Difficult times can bring beautiful stories that bring joy and hope to others. What is your story doing?

December 21

I have also seen this example of wisdom under the sun, and it seemed great to me (Ecclesiastes 9:13, ESV).

Did You Know

Did you know…1 in 5 children in the United States live in poverty?
Did you know…every 10 seconds, a child is reported abused or neglected?
Did you know…that nearly 31 million Americans live in hunger or on the verge of going to bed hungry every night?
Did you know…That one out of every 6 senior citizens live at or near the poverty line?
Did you know…that on any given night, several hundred thousand people in America are without a home and that 37% of them are families with children?
Did you know…that 2 million people in the United States are incarcerated, more than three times the number just 20 years ago? Did you know many of them have small children?

Did you know…that every day VOA is working to make a positive difference in their lives?

There are no limits to caring ®

December 22

In this world you will have trouble. But take heart! I have overcome the world (John 16:33, NIV).

Hard Times

Many people are anxious. Worried about the economy, worried about losing jobs, or not being able to pay the bills. Many people are worried about finances and being able to take care of their employees and the people they serve. Hard times are here for many. Most people are being affected in one way or another.

Recently, a grandmother was talking with her grandson, Matthew, about hard times. "Hard times are coming," she told Matthew. "I don't know what we are going to do." She went on to say. "One thing is for sure: this Christmas, there won't be any presents under the tree."

Being the understanding child that Matthew is, he said, "That's okay, grandma, a gift card will be fine."

These times may require more adjusting. They may require sacrifice… a change in our lifestyle. Times may be hard and uncertain at the moment, but we have our family, our loved ones. That is the greatest gift of all.

December 23

In my observation of people's burdens here on earth, I discovered that there is ceaseless activity, day and night (Ecclesiastes 8:16, NLT).

Buy Your Own Gift

Last Christmas, John was feeling his age and found that shopping for Christmas gifts had become too difficult. So instead, he sends checks to everyone.

In each card, he wrote, "Buy your own gift!" and mailed them early. He enjoyed the usual flurry of family festivities, and it was only after the holiday that he noticed that he had received very few cards in return.

Puzzled over this, he went into his study, intending to write a couple of his relatives and ask what had happened. It was then that he got his answer. Under a stack of papers, he was horrified to find the checks which he had forgotten to enclose with the cards.

Christmas is the busiest season of the year. Take time to slow down and enjoy the season while being a blessing to others!

December 24

Give, and it will be given to you. Good measure, pressed down, shaken together, running over (Luke 6:38, ESV).

Truck Stop

A young woman finally made up her mind to leave an abusive husband. With six kids and just a few dollars in her pocket, she headed for a new life.

She searched and finally convinced the owner of a truck stop to give her a waitress job. Every night, she and the kids knelt down and thanked God for getting Mommy a job.

However, she was working six nights a week and still couldn't make ends meet. As Christmas approached, heating bills were rising. The kids had no toys or clothes for Christmas.

On Christmas Eve, the usual customers were drinking coffee at the truck stop. When it was time for her to go home, she was amazed to find her car filled with boxes of all shapes and sizes. Clothes, candy, groceries, and more!

You see, there were angels that night… at that truck stop. You, too, can be an angel.

December 25

For to us a child is born, to us a son is given (Isaiah 9:6, ESV).

Big Speech

Sometimes big speeches are given in little places. After WWII, Winston Churchill came to America and gave a speech in a small Missouri town. In that speech, he coined the term "Iron Curtain." That term, and that speech, will live forever in the history of the world.

Two thousand years ago, in a small, secluded town called Bethlehem, God issued a speech that will live for all time and eternity. "For unto you is born this day in the city of David, a Savior, who is Christ the Lord."

The subject of that speech is the reason for this season. And today, we celebrate the love and peace that Jesus brought into the world. "For God so loved the world, that He gave…"

We at VOA Southeast wish you a Merry Christmas and hope that you have the joy of Christmas – the joy that comes from giving out of a sense of gratitude because you have learned there are no limits to caring.

December 26

It is good to give thanks (Psalm 82:1, ESV).

Grandma's Christmas Strategy

One Christmas, a mother decided she was no longer going to remind her adult kids to send thank you notes. Consequently, the kids' grandmother never received any thanks for the Christmas checks she sent to the kids.

The very next Christmas, all the kids stopped by in person to thank their grandmother for their check.

When asked by a friend about this change in behavior, the grandmother replied, "Simple. This year I didn't sign the checks."

Wow…sometimes we need to simply say "thank you." Maybe we could even write a thank you note…with a stamp. Perhaps that's out of date!

Or is it? Is expressing thanks to one another or God out of date?

No, you can't text God or write a note…but through prayer you can say "thank you." Now write your Grandmother a thank you note and mail it. I wish I could!

December 27

Esau ran to meet him and embraced him and fell on his neck and kissed him (Genesis 33:4, ESV).

Christmas Hug

On the day of the school Christmas party, little Jenny approached her teacher and asked if she would be offended that she didn't give her a Christmas present.

The teacher told her, "No, I know you have a Christmas present for me." But Jenny said, "No, we don't have any money. My daddy got drunk, so we have no money, and Santa Claus isn't coming."

The teacher replied, "But I know you have the very best present of all for me, and you've been saving it for last." Little Jenny looked up at her teacher, puzzled. The teacher said, "I'm ready for my Christmas hug…I know you have a hug for me."

The rest of the day, Jenny told all the other students that she had given her teacher the best present of the day…a Christmas hug.

Did you get the gift you wanted for Christmas? Maybe, maybe not. But the best gifts are given with love and kindness – like a hug.

December 28

It is my eager expectation and hope that I will not be at all ashamed (Philippians 1:20, ESV).

Perfect Holidays

So how are you doing these holidays? Did you have a white Christmas just like the ones you used to know? Did you do what everyone expected? Or what you expected?

Willie Nelson said, "I always do what I'm expected to do, except when I don't."

There are times when we place unrealistic expectations on ourselves. None of us can perform perfectly. And things around us don't always come out perfect... And particularly around Christmas and holidays we want things to be perfect...like we remembered they used to be.

When we cannot capture the past or fix things that are broken, can we still enjoy the moment?

Sometimes we have to let self-imposed expectations go...those great Christmases of the past...well, they too were not perfect.

However, expectations are not all bad. They can motivate us to good behavior and better performance.

December 29

A joyful heart is a good medicine (Proverbs 17:22, ESV).

Contagious Flu

We have had a tough winter, and many have had the flu! And many have spread the flu to others. At least one entire school closed down for two days because the flu was contagious! Not good to catch!

But there are some contagious things that are worth catching.
- A smile is contagious. Just carry a smile, and others around you will smile too.
- How about being a carrier of encouragement? We could sure use an epidemic of positive encouragement.
- How about being a carrier of hope or peace? We could certainly use an outbreak of hope and peace.
- Wouldn't it be wonderful to infect others with love and kindness? Kind acts can be spread far and wide without any containment.

These infections make us well, not sick. Today, you can be a carrier of a smile, an encouraging word, peace, and an act of kindness. Be contagious!

December 30

Pay to all what is owed to them . . . respect to whom respect is owed, honor to whom honor is owed (Romans 13:7, ESV).

Deer Hunter

A hunter and his friend were sitting in a tree stand in the woods near the highway one cold morning. Suddenly, a huge buck walked out of the corn. It was magnificent.

The hunter's hand shook with excitement. Moving quickly, he carefully aimed the scope on his gun at the unsuspecting buck. As he was about to squeeze the trigger on this deer of a lifetime, his friend alerted him to a funeral procession passing slowly down the highway.

The hunter set the rifle down and prayed. His friend was stunned, "Wow, that is the most thoughtful and touching thing I have ever seen you do. You actually let that trophy deer go to pay respects to a passing funeral procession. You are the kindest man I have ever known."

The hunter shrugged. "Yeah, well, we were married for 37 years."

Kindness is more about how you treat your spouse than anyone else.

December 31

Oh, sing to the LORD a new song, for he has done marvelous things! (Psalm 98:1, ESV).

Try Again

Did you succeed at everything you attempted this year? I know I didn't. If you didn't, try again. Don't give up. Only through persistence can you achieve worthwhile objectives.

The author of Dr. Seuss took his first book to 20 publishers before succeeding. Inventor Thomas Edison often made as many as 50,000 attempts before coming up with a workable product. Abraham Lincoln lost most of his political races before being elected President of the United States. Babe Ruth struck out 1330 times.

Very few successful people start out with success. Success comes to those who persist. Often it comes to those who first fail but keep on trying.

Don't quit. Go after your dreams. You are the only one who can make them come true. Don't quit. Try again. If at first you don't succeed, try, try again.

There are no limits to caring ®

About the Author

Wallace T. Davis is a graduate of Samford University and New Orleans Baptist Theological Seminary with a Bachelor of Science in Education, a Master of Theology, and a Doctor of Philosophy in Psychology and Counseling.

Wallace served as pastor, teacher, counselor, keynote speaker, and Chief Executive Officer, spanning over 50 years. For 42 years, he has been with Volunteers of America. In 1980, with the founding of Volunteers of America in Mobile, he became the first Community Board President and, shortly afterwards, the first Executive Director. As President and Chief Executive Officer, he led the organization to expand and serve Alabama, Georgia, and Mississippi addressing some of the most challenging spiritual, social, and economic issues of our time.

Wallace and his wife Barbara have four adult children and nine grandchildren.

Permissions for Bible Translations Used

NIV Scriptures marked (NIV) are taken from the Holy Bible, New International Version®, NIV®. Copyright © 1973, 1978, 1984, 2011 by Biblica, Inc.™ Used by permission of Zondervan. All rights reserved worldwide. www.zondervan.com The "NIV" and "New International Version" are trademarks registered in the United States Patent and Trademark Office by Biblica, Inc.®

ESV Scripture quotations marked (ESV) are from the ESV® Bible (The Holy Bible, English Standard Version®), copyright© 2001 by Crossway Bibles, a publishing ministry of Good News Publishers. Used by permission. All rights reserved.

NLT Scripture quotations marked (NLT) are taken from the Holy Bible, New Living Translation, copyright ©1996, 2004, 2015 by Tyndale House Foundation. Used by permission of Tyndale House Publishers, a Division of Tyndale House Ministries, Carol Stream, Illinois 60188. All rights reserved.

CEV Scripture quotations marked (CEV) are from the Contemporary English Version Copyright © 1991, 1992, 1995 by American Bible Society, Used by Permission.

TLB Scripture quotations marked (TLB) are taken from The Living Bible copyright © 1971. Used by permission of Tyndale House Publishers, a Division of Tyndale House Ministries, Carol Stream, Illinois 60188. All rights reserved.

MSG Scripture quotations marked MSG are taken from *THE MESSAGE*, copyright © 1993, 2002, 2018 by Eugene H. Peterson. Used by permission of NavPress. All rights reserved. Represented by Tyndale House Publishers, a Division of Tyndale House Ministries.

NKJV Scripture taken from the New King James Version®. Copyright © 1982 by Thomas Nelson. Used by permission. All rights reserved.

Made in the USA
Columbia, SC
28 April 2025